MW01289828

Beginner Marathoner's Faith Training

How to Become a Supernatural Runner

By Alla Hatfield

ALLA HATFIELD

Copyright © 2012 Alla Hatfield

All Rights Reserved

Cover design by Jason Oakman, Xsalta LLC

"Compelling, practical, and incisive, this is the definitive guide on how to build your "faith training" while you pursue your first marathon! This book will be kept right next to my training schedule!"

Frank Zaffino
Instructor of Kinesiology, The Pennsylvania State University
Athletic Trainer Certified
Performance Enhancement Specialist
Age-group Marathoner and Endurance Athlete

"Alla's book is all about winning the race of Life. Your faith will soar as you read and apply the principles she shares to everyday life! The powerful daily truths will inspire you to "draw" from the supernatural ability available to you and walk with God on a higher level. Are you ready? On your mark, get set, go!"

Brian Wills
Founder, Healing for the Nations
Author, *10 Hours to Live*

To my husband Dave. No matter what life brings, I am thankful we are in this race together.

To my parents Valentina and Nikolai. You've set a great pace for my run by your own example.

To my mentors George and Donna Snow. You've touched so many lives. I am honored to carry your baton!

BEGINNER MARATHONER'S FAITH TRAINING

TABLE OF CONTENTS

DAY 1 (Long Run 8 miles*) CRAVING FREEDOM
DAY 2 (Short Run 3 miles) "RUN IN SUCH A WAY…"
DAY 3 (Rest Day, Meditation) MEDITATING FROM GOD'S PERSPECTIVE
DAY 4 (Short Run, Speed Training 4 miles) PUSHING THROUGH
Day 5 (Short Run 4 miles) THE STARTING LINE
Day 6 (Short Run 4 miles) A CALL ACCORDING TO HIS PURPOSE
Day 7 (Rest Day, Meditation) MEDITATING FROM GOD'S PERSPECTIVE AGAIN

Day 1 (Long Run 8 miles) A CALL TESTED
Day 2 (Short Run 4 miles) POINTS OF REFERENCE
Day 3 (Rest Day, Meditation) PEACE OF MIND
Day 4 (Short Run, Speed Training 4 miles) A BIGGER PICTURE
Day 5 (Short Run 4 miles) THE FLASHING NUMBERS
Day 6 (Short Run 4 miles) REPLACING BROKEN PARTS
Day 7 (Rest Day, Meditation) THE WORK OF RESTORATION-

Day 1 (Long Run 10 miles) A DAILY TRAINING MINIMUM?
Day 2 (Short Run 4 miles) HYDRATE
Day 3 (Rest Day) REST
Day 4 (Short Run, Speed Training 4 miles) GAIN MUSCLE
Day 5 (Short Run 4 miles) EAT WELL

Day 6 (Short Run 4 miles) INCREASE GRADUALLY
Day 7 (Rest Day, Meditation) PUT ONE FOOT IN FRONT OF
THE OTHER

Day 1 (Long Run 8 miles) BREAKING FREE
Day 2 (Short Run 4 miles) RUNNING TO OR RUNNING
FROM?
Day 3 (Rest and Meditation) FORGIVNESS
Day 4 (Short Run, Speed Training 4 miles) A NEW
STANDARD
Day 5 (Short Run 4 miles) MENTALITY OF TRUST
Day 6 (Short Run 4 miles) FEARLESS LOVE
Day 7 (Rest Day, Meditation) LET THE HEALING BEGIN

Day 1 (Long Run 13 miles) DETERMINE YOUR "ZONE"
Day 2 (Short Run 3 miles) GUIDED BY HIS VOICE
Day 3 (Rest Day, Meditation) UNDERSTANDING THE WILL
OF GOD
Day 4 (Short Run, Speed Training 4 miles) FEELING GOD'S
HEARTBEAT
Day 5 (Short Run 5 miles) GOD AT WORK
Day 6 (Short Run 4 miles) OBEDIENCE
Day 7 (Rest Day, Meditation) WHAT IF I MISS IT?

Day 1 (Long Run 10 miles) FATHER'S LOVE
Day 2 (Short Run 4 miles) RUN TO THE FATHER
Day 3 (Rest Day, Meditation) FATHER'S IMAGE
Day 4 (Short Run, Speed Training 4 miles) INTIMACY IN
FATHER'S ARMS
Day 5 (Short Run 4 miles) FROM ORPHANS TO SONS

Day 6 (Short Run 4 miles) NAMED BY THE FATHER
Day 7 (Rest Day, Meditation) LOVE NEVER FAILS

Day 1 (Long Run 15 miles) IT HAPPENS TO THE BEST OF US
Day 2 (Short Run 3 miles) WILL TO GET BACK UP
Day 3 (Rest Day, Meditation) LOOKING PAST THE HURT
AND EMBARRASMENT
Day 4 (Short Run, Speed Training 5 miles) KICKING INTO A
HIGHER GEAR
Day 5 (Short Run 5 miles) BURSTING PAST YOUR
OPPONENTS
Day 6 (Short Run 4 miles) SEIZING YOUR OPPORTUNITY
Day 7 (Rest Day, Meditation) FINISHING IN VICTORY

Day 1 (Long Run 12 miles) NO MOUNTAIN HIGH, NO
VALLEY LOW
Day 2 (Short Run 4 miles) LIKE THE FEET OF A DEER
Day 3 (Rest Day, Meditation) KILLER HILL, IS IT WORTH IT?
Day 4 (Short Run, Speed Training 4 miles) CONDITIONED
FOR HILLS
Day 5 (Short Run 4 miles) MOUNTAINS AND VALLEYS
INSIDE OF US
Day 6 (Short Run 4 miles) PLACES OF REVELATION
Day 7 (Rest Day, Meditation) THE VIEW FROM THE TOP

DAY 1 (Long Run 18 miles) THE FIRST RELAY LEG
Day 2 (Short Run 3 miles) PART OF A TEAM
Day 3 (Rest Day, Meditation) FROM GENERATION TO
GENERATION

Day 1 (Long Run 13 miles) ACCORDING TO HIS POWER
WITHIN US
Day 2 (Short Run 6 miles) STINKING THINKING?
Day 3 (Rest Day, Meditation) THE MIND OF CHRIST
Day 4 (Short Run, Speed Training 6 miles) WHAT ABOUT
POSITIVE TALKING?
Day 5 (Short Run 5 miles) THINK BY FAITH
Day 6 (Short Run 5 miles) QUESTIONING HEAVEN
Day 7 (Short Run 4 miles, Meditation) GODLY WISDOM
THAT WORKS

Day 1 (Long Run 20 miles) DON'T SETTLE FOR THE
MEDIOCRE
Day 2 (Short Run 3 miles) PERFECTIONISM
Day 3 (Rest Day, Meditation) BETTER IS ONE DAY IN YOUR
COURTS
Day 4 (Short Run, Speed Training 6 miles) DON'T
DISREGARD YOUR FIRST MILE
Day 5 (Short Run 5 miles) LUCKY OR BLESSED?
Day 6 (Short Run 6 miles) MORE PRECIOUS THAN GOLD
Day 7 (Rest Day, Meditation) I WILL COME FORTH AS GOLD

Day 1 (Long Run 13 miles) IN HIM
Day 2 (Short Run 6 miles) SUPERNATURAL RUNNERS
Day 3 (Rest Day, Meditation) CHILDREN OF GOD
Day 4 (Short Run 4 miles, Speed Training) MORE THAN
CONQUERORS
Day 5 (Short Run 4 miles) SAINTS
Day 6 (Short Run 4 miles) GOD'S WORKMANSHIP
Day 7 (Short Run 4 miles, Meditation) THE MISSING LINK

Day 1 (Long Run 20 miles) THE LAST 20-MILER AND THE
CALL TESTED AGAIN
Day 2 (Rest Day, Meditation) WATCHING OUT FOR INJURIES
Day 3 (Short Run 4 miles) BEYOND YOUR COMFORT ZONE
Day 4 (Short Run, Speed Training 4 miles) ON TIRED LEGS
Day 5 (Short Run 3 miles) DON'T FORGET TO BREATHE
Day 6 (Short Run 4 miles) POP IN THAT POWER GEL
Day 7 (Rest Day, Meditation) DETERMINED TO SUCCEED

Day 1 (Long Run 15 miles) WHAT'S A RUNNER'S HIGH?
Day 2 (Short Run 3 miles) IT BRINGS TRANSFORMATION
Day 3 (Rest Day, Meditation) IT MAKES US RESPOND IN
PRAISE
Day 4 (Short Run, Speed Training 5 miles) IT BRINGS
REFRESHING
Day 5 (Short Run 4 miles) PLACE OF PEACE
Day 6 (Short Run 5 miles) PLACE OF JOY
Day 7 (Rest Day, Meditation) LOVING WITH ALL YOUR
PASSION

DAY 1 (A Short "Long" Run 4 miles) A CRAMP IN MY SIDE
Day 2 (Short Run 6 miles) KEEP IT GOING
Day 3 (Rest Day, Meditation) YOU ARE A REFLECTION OF
HIS DELIVERANCE
Day 4 (Short Run 4 miles, no speed training today) YOU ARE
AN OVERCOMER
Day 5 (Short Run 4 miles) YOU ARE A LIGHT ON A HILL
DAY 6 (Rest Day, Meditation) YOU ARE YOKED WITH HIM
Day 7 (Short Run, 2 miles) YOU ARE HIS VICTORIOUS BRIDE
YOUR BIG DAY (26.2!)

INTRODUCTION OR A PRE-RACE HYDRATION

My Dear Reader,

Do you feel like your life is a long endurance race, or has it been more of a relaxing jog so far? No matter how you might answer this question right now, and whether you've never run a mile or you live and breathe running, from now on I will be calling you "My Dear Marathoner." You rightfully deserve a title like this because I believe in many ways living life is like running a marathon, although at times it can be so challenging and complex that it might look more like an Ironman or a Tough Mudder. But let's just start with a marathon. I am not an athletic expert by any means. You will not find many practical tips on running in this book. There are plenty of other resources out there if you are looking for advice on physical training. Instead, I would like to share some of my inspirations that apply running principles to every day living. I hope they will challenge and boost your mental and spiritual performance on real running tracks and, even more so, on the trails of life. If you are a runner, this book is for you because it will motivate you beyond your physical goals. If you are not a runner, this book is written for you as well: it will unveil the training principles you could use to become a supernatural runner in your life's journey.

Who is a "supernatural runner?" If I could sum up my own definition, it would be a person who has the tenacity to press into the realm of God by faith in order to grasp everything God has for her. A "supernatural runner" doesn't settle for the mundane and mediocre and goes for God's gold. It's a person who is desperate to fulfill her divinely-given purpose. As a result, she gets to see God's grace and favor released upon her life above and beyond what is naturally possible. My ambition is that these words will one day fully describe me. It would be nice if I could just wing a marathon, but I realize I need to train myself physically in order to finish it and run well without any injuries. In the same way, I need to train myself in faith in order to run the race of life farther and faster than I ever dreamed or imagined. If you would like the words "supernatural runner" to characterize you in any way, I encourage you to set out with me on this training journey.

The idea to write this devotional was conceived on a treadmill during the end of my 13.1 mile run. (You can only imagine what kind of things come to one's mind when she is huffing and puffing in front of a treadmill monitor for two hours!) I did amazingly well by my standards, completing a distance of a half marathon at an 8:35 minute per mile pace. For some of you runners this might sound like nothing, but I had never run that long of a distance that fast in my life. As soon as I got off the treadmill I registered for the Pittsburgh Marathon and picked up a pen and paper.

I wish I could say I have some credentials to my name that enable me to write this book. I'm not an Olympic champion; I don't even qualify for Boston. I'm just an average person that gets a deep sense of significance from accomplishing a long distance course and from experiencing God's purposes released through my life. I am writing this to prove that if *I* can train for a marathon and finish it, *you* don't have to be a spiritual superstar to fulfill God's call on your life.

This devotional, just like the marathon training schedule I am about to attempt, is a 17 week faith training challenge that consists of a combination of long runs (long readings), short runs (short readings), and rest days (meditation days) that will zero you in on fulfilling your life's destiny. If you dare to accept it, we will train and run this course together. We will tackle the race of life from a faith perspective. I have no idea what lies ahead of us but I am putting on my running shoes. Will you join me?

Week 1: A CALL TO RUN

DAY 1 (Long Run 8 miles*) CRAVING FREEDOM

We run, not because we think it is doing us good, but because we enjoy it and cannot help ourselves... The more restricted our society and work become, the more necessary it will be to find some outlet for this craving for freedom. No one can say "You must not run faster than this, or jump higher than that." The human spirit is indomitable. – Roger Bannister, first runner to break the 4-minute mile[1]

God gives the Spirit without limit. – John 3:34b (NIV)[2]

Roger Bannister nailed it. To put his quote in spiritual terms, true running in faith can never be fueled by religious obligation. Dry and lifeless religion of "do's and don'ts" will only limit you. If you've ever started a diet or an exercise program and quit before you reached your goal you can relate to the fact that if you try to do anything in life just because "it's good for you," you won't experience a lasting change. The challenge of this book is to come to the place where you pursue God because you enjoy him and cannot help doing so. Once you come to the realization that God is the true source of the freedom you really crave, then no one will be able to say to you that you may not experience God deeper than this, or see His work in your life farther than that. The apostle John reveals the key to breaking the spiritual four minute mile barrier in your life: "God gives the Spirit without limit."

Most people I know would say they hope to realize their full potential in life. This drive is so natural and common that it sounds like a cliché. However, it really speaks of our innate desire to fulfill God's call on our lives. I believe God's purpose for you is never small or insignificant. In fact, the "running" course He prepared for you is of such unfathomable distance and sometimes requires such speed that you could never accomplish it by your own strength and talent. The only way to succeed in such a race is to rely on His supernatural ability placed upon you through your faith in Christ. You train for physical runs in the natural and you get what you train for. In the same way, you learn to grow in your faith by exercising it and by connecting to the Source of your spiritual strength. You get as much of God as you believe you can have.

Whatever challenges you are facing right now, whatever dreams or desires you have for your life, keep in mind that you always have two choices. One is to accomplish things on your own and the other is to accept the challenge of living by faith in God's power.

My Dear Marathoner, meditate on the questions below throughout the day or on your long run. Write the answers down when you can.

Questions to ponder: What are some of your goals and dreams that require more than your own personal ability to accomplish? In what areas of your life has God been stirring up your faith?

*If you are planning to follow my mileage suggestions for your runs, you need to establish a running baseline of an average 20-22 miles per week with long runs averaging 6-8 miles once a week for at least a few months before beginning the actual marathon training.

Week 1: A CALL TO RUN

DAY 2 (Short Run 3 miles) "RUN IN SUCH A WAY..."

Do you not know that in a race all the runners run, but only one gets the prize? Run in such a way as to get the prize. – 1 Corinthians 9:24 (NIV)

The verse quoted above is one of the most famous "running" scriptures in the Bible. Even though it seems to focus on the finish line and the reward, I would like to draw your attention to the "Run in such a way..." part. I appreciate the fact that when I run marathons I get a participant medal regardless of whether I finish first or last. For me, it is always an accomplishment just to complete it. In the same way, we all eventually get to the finish line in the race of life. It's *how* we run our course that should be important to us right now. The *how* shows the character we display on our run, the way we treat others, the manner in which we approach obstacles. Is our life primarily marked by joy, peace, and thankfulness, or by disappointment, frustration, and depression? In order to win in a physical race, we not only need to give our best effort but also to be able to endure and maintain a steady pace. Likewise, in our spiritual journey, we are all called to give it our best shot and sustain our faith throughout its course. There is no place for quitting because of spiritual fatigue.

Recently, I got in touch with an old friend of mine who is a good athlete. He was impressed to find out that I had done two marathons and that I was training for another one. He told me that once during his college years he participated in one on a dare without any training. The last five miles he dragged on shaking legs and then could barely walk for several days. He never entered another marathon. His finish time and mine were very similar. However, I enjoyed my experience despite the tough physical challenge. He barely made it and hated every step of the way, at least during the second half of the race.

My Dear Marathoner, what you decide to do with God's call on your life will determine how you train and in what manner you race to the finish line. If you want God do great things through your life you will train hard in your faith run. If you want to be a "supernatural" runner, you will need to train and run your course relying on the power of the Holy Spirit, at times disregarding both your own strengths and weaknesses. As you submit to God and strive after His purposes, you can be sure that through the power of the Holy Spirit you will finish in first place. You won't just get a finisher's medal; you'll proudly receive the champion's prize!

Week 1: A CALL TO RUN

DAY 3 (Rest Day, Meditation) MEDITATING FROM GOD'S PERSPECTIVE

Set your minds on things above, not on earthly things. —
Colossians 3:2 (NIV)

My Dear Marathoner, please do not disregard your rest days. It is recommended that you take breaks from running in order to prevent injury and allow your muscles to recover. However, as athletes know, a rest day does not mean you do nothing. Many runners do stretching and strength training on rest days. Some cross train and do biking or swimming. I must confess though that as a full time mom of two young children with a part time job I get caught up in errands and various little things I do for my family on the days I rest from running.

In this devotional, our rest days will involve some prayer, meditation, and Scripture reading. Take your eyes off of the running track. Try not to focus on your circumstances and performance. Be still and hear what God is speaking to your heart. This is often the hardest thing to do, especially if you are going through a crisis or have been waiting for an answer to prayer for a long time. I believe that in order to run the race well you need these still moments to get God's perspective on how He sees you and your circumstances.

Scripture to meditate on: *Call to me and I will answer you and tell you great and unsearchable things you do not know."* – *Jeremiah 33:3 (NIV)*

Meditation and prayer:

What areas of my life does God want me to focus on during this "training" season? Ask God to reveal Himself to you in those areas and build your faith through reading this devotional.

Week 1: A CALL TO RUN

DAY 4 (Short Run, Speed Training 4 miles) PUSHING THROUGH

The secret of endurance is to remember that your pain is temporary but your reward will be eternal. — Rick Warren, The Purpose Driven Life[3]

Many long distant runners do at least one speed training run per week. A speed training run involves varying your speed during repeated time or distance increments. At times you run at a comfortable pace, but at other points you accelerate and push yourself to the limit. I would much rather go on a long leisurely run than have a short difficult workout like this, but experts say it is effective. In a way, this is how life is. Sometimes everything is peaceful and familiar, and at other times we are thrown out of our comfort zone and all we can do is push through. When you are pushing yourself to the limit, that's when you want to stop the most. You start questioning yourself and doubting whether you will ever arrive at the finish line. During that time, it is important to remember that those speed and distance increments don't last forever. Things will eventually slow down and become easier. On the other hand, conquering those peaks will give you confidence and stamina. When challenges arise again, you will have a testimony of victory, a testimony of His power in your life.

In the speed workouts I would like to challenge you to get out of your comfort zone and dare to reach for God in ways you haven't before. Today my challenge to you is to pray a prayer of commitment to engage in the training of your faith.

Week 1: A CALL TO RUN

Day 5 (Short Run 4 miles) THE STARTING LINE

And we have seen and testify that the Father has sent his Son to be the Savior of the world. If anyone acknowledges that Jesus is the Son of God, God lives in him and he in God. And so we know and rely on the love God has for us. — 1 John 4:14-16 (NIV)

My Dear Marathoner, this is where the starting line lies. Understanding and accepting the love of God is the point we need to get to before we even attempt the race. We might have to linger there for quite a bit until we truly grasp the freeing reality of having a Heavenly Daddy whose love we can rely on completely every step of the way.

Most people struggle to find the starting line. Sadly enough, many actually confuse it with the finish. They think that they obtain the Father's love and approval only if they perform well and finish the race. This misunderstanding of God's nature is deeply rooted in our negative childhood experiences and cold religious rules.

The love of God is what defines our call. The love of God is what sustains us during the race. If you've never experienced this love before, today is the day to start. Ask Jesus to be your personal Savior: "Jesus, I come to You today asking You to become the Lord and Savior of my life. Thank you for dying on the cross for my sin. Please forgive me and help me live for You. I want to know You and have a relationship with You. Help me run the race of life the way You intended me to. Thank you Jesus for saving me! Amen." Congratulations, your run has just begun! I pray God the Father would reveal to you and me the depths of His love.

Week 1: A CALL TO RUN

Day 6 (Short Run 4 miles) A CALL ACCORDING TO HIS PURPOSE

And we know that in all things God works for the good of those who love him, who have been called according to his purpose. —
Romans 8:28 (NIV)

Your life has a purpose. Before you were even born God had mapped out the course you were going to run. This course is a part of His sovereign plan on the earth. You get to choose whether you want to run it according to His purposes and under the mantle of His Lordship and protection. This is why the Bible talks about the "hope" of our calling in Ephesians 1:18-19: "I pray also that the eyes of your heart may be enlightened in order that you may know the hope to which he has called you, the riches of his glorious inheritance in the saints, and his incomparably great power for us who believe." The call is not forced on us; we decide to respond to it out of our love for Him because He first loved us. Whether you're the President of the United States or a stay at home mom, you have significance and value in the context of His hope and plan, which is "Christ in you" according to Colossians 1:27: "To them God has chosen to make known among the Gentiles the glorious riches of this mystery, which is Christ in you, the hope of glory." Maybe you are going through a divorce, your business is plummeting down, or your loved one is sick. Whatever adversity you are going through right now, know that He will hold you in His hand and work things out for your good because your life has a purpose. God will keep you on the right track even though it may be hard to see how that might be possible.

Week 1: A CALL TO RUN

Day 7 (Rest Day, Meditation) MEDITATING FROM GOD'S PERSPECTIVE AGAIN

For as he thinks in his heart, so is he. — Proverbs 23:7 (NKJV)[4]

Athletes are encouraged to visualize themselves performing their event. Sometimes during my training I imagine myself running strong and steady on the streets of my marathon course. It inspires me to pursue my goal. It also helps me during the actual race to feel the way I had envisioned myself. What do you think about yourself in your heart? How do you view yourself and your life? The way you see yourself is the way you will be. It is so important to merge your self-image with the way God sees you and to believe what He says about you in order to fulfill your life's destiny. God gave you an imagination to be used in a powerful way. You can actively engage it to visualize yourself successfully pursuing God's purposes by faith.

Meditation and prayer:

How often do you think of yourself from God's perspective, as loved, forgiven, cleansed, and empowered by the Holy Spirit? How often do you think of yourself based on your past failures, present limitations, and uncertainty of the future? All day today try to imagine yourself successfully walking out God's call on your life. Do not allow yourself to engage in negative self-talk. Reflect at the end of the day: do you feel any different? My prayer today is "Father, teach me to see myself the way You see me."

Week 2: WHEN YOUR TREADMILL BREAKS

Day 1 (Long Run 8 miles) A CALL TESTED

Your treadmill is designed to be reliable and easy to use.
However, if you experience a problem, please reference the
troubleshooting guide listed below. — Treadmill User's Guide

How ironic is it that as I am about to train for a marathon and write a book on training in faith, my treadmill decided to break down? As I was running at the highest speed interval, it suddenly made a strange creaking sound, stumbled, and stopped. I tried to push buttons but nothing worked. When my husband came home and opened the "hood," he discovered that one of the important parts of the motor was bent. We called the company to replace the part and now we're waiting for it to come in the mail.

Very often as you commit to step it up, things that you think are essential in accomplishing your mission start to malfunction. What happens when you encounter obstacles? What do you do when life unexpectedly throws you off the running belt and refuses to move the way it did before? Maybe you've lost a loved one. Maybe you've lost your job. Maybe you were rejected or got sick? If you have anything left in you, you try to push familiar faith buttons but they don't seem to work. What happens to your call in that case? Maybe you are asking yourself, "why is my faith that had been running so smoothly suddenly not working?" Is there a way to open the "hood" and get to the core?

In the case of my treadmill, I couldn't get it to move until I got the help of the manufacturer and had the part of the motor replaced. God is our Creator. He has the troubleshooting guide and will show us what the real problem is. He can fix our broken parts. Ask for His help and the help of His family.

In the meantime, running outside is my only choice. Don't get me wrong; I prefer running outside to the treadmill, but not when it is below freezing. I went out anyway and had to admit that it was not so bad despite the fact that it was the end of December in Pennsylvania. When presented with the choice of not running or running in the freezing cold I still chose running. Why? Thank you for asking. I did it not because I had to but out of my love for running and my commitment to train.

Question to ponder throughout the day or on your long run: Are there any "malfunctions" in your life that you feel stand in between you and fulfilling God's call? How do you think they should be handled? Ask God for His wisdom. Father, I pray you would remove anything (try to be specific) in my life that slows me down by being more important to me than You. Please restore the areas of my life that have been "malfunctioning."

Week 2: WHEN YOUR TREADMILL BREAKS

Day 2 (Short Run 4 miles) POINTS OF REFERENCE

Let the word of Christ dwell in you richly... — Colossians 3:16a
(NIV)

One of the reasons to miss running on the treadmill is that it does a nice job of pacing you and showing you the exact stats of your run, such as speed, incline level, calories burned, and time left in your workout. I can somewhat judge how I am doing when I run outside, especially if I wear a stop watch, but I can never be as consistent and precise as when I rely on the treadmill monitor. In some marathons there are "pacers" who help you make sure that if you keep up with them you will finish at your goal time.

I wish there was a monitor in life that constantly told us how we are doing and what "mile markers" we have achieved so far. The truth of God's word that we find in the Bible is the perfect point of reference for us. We might live relying on our feelings and think we are running a seven minute mile when in fact we are managing only a nine minute per mile pace. On the contrary, we might be hard on ourselves thinking that we are being too slow or that our running form is bad when in reality God is pleased and wants us to enjoy the process. When we base our life on the truth of God's word and allow the Holy Spirit to lead us, we learn exactly what God has to say about each turn and segment of our life's course. Having His word and His Spirit inside of us is like having a built-in monitor that helps us evaluate and sustain our pace.

Week 2: WHEN YOUR TREADMILL BREAKS

Day 3 (Rest Day, Meditation) PEACE OF MIND

Do not be anxious about anything, but in everything, by prayer and petition, with thanksgiving, present your requests to God. And the peace of God, which transcends all understanding, will guard your hearts and your minds in Christ Jesus. — Philippians 4:6-7 (NIV)

These verses talk about giving our worries to God in prayer with thanksgiving. There is a reason why thanksgiving is important in our petitions to God. It seals our trust and confidence in the fact that God is not just able but is also willing to meet our need. When we have that kind of trust, we have peace that cannot be explained by our external circumstances. Where there is lack of peace there is lack of trust. Even though I am anxious to have my treadmill fixed I choose to trust that God will not let what happened sabotage my training and, ultimately, my race.

Meditation and Prayer:

When you consider things that are "broken" in your life right now, do you have peace that God will not let them affect the outcome of your life? Do you have confidence that He will take care of the problem? If you don't have peace, then talk to God and ask Him to help you to trust Him. Then make a conscious decision to rely on Him in the midst of your difficult circumstances, thanking Him that He will see you through. Ask the Holy Spirit to give you His supernatural peace.

Week 2: WHEN YOUR TREADMILL BREAKS

Day 4 (Short Run, Speed Training 4 miles) A BIGGER PICTURE

Have the courage to live under strain and pain to be part of a better story. A larger story. Don't wimp out. — Beth Moore, James. Mercy Triumphs[5]

I almost wimped out in the face of the bone chilling wind today but I wanted to be on pace with my training schedule. I got my butt outside and ran. It wasn't just about me going on a jog anymore. It was about being a part of an exciting big race several months down the road.

When you submit yourself to God's call you realize that your life is not about enjoying a leisurely stroll anymore. It is not about you, period. Both you and I have a chance to be a part of something very important and thrilling that God has planned. This thought gives me the inspiration to look past my own strains and discomfort. I hope that seeing your life in the larger context of God's plan will motivate you to keep going strong as well.

Week 2: WHEN YOUR TREADMILL BREAKS

Day 5 (Short Run 4 miles) THE FLASHING NUMBERS

I consider that our present sufferings are not worth comparing with the glory that will be revealed in us. — Romans 8:18 (NIV)

As I wrote in Day 3 of this week, having a consistent point of reference can be helpful but it can also be detrimental. Those of you who have run on a treadmill or use any kind of cardio exercise equipment know what I am talking about. If you constantly look down at the monitor to see how much time or how many miles you have left, it feels like time goes by extremely slowly. All of a sudden, it seems like your workout is taking forever and it's never going to end.

Even though an accurate evaluation is important in training, you can't do it all the time. If you constantly look at your performance, engaging in meticulous self-analysis and comparisons, you will inevitably get discouraged. If you can't help but glance at the flashing numbers on the monitor, make sure you focus on how well you've done and how far God has brought you, not on how far you still need to go.

Week 2: WHEN YOUR TREADMILL BREAKS

Day 6 (Short Run 4 miles) REPLACING BROKEN PARTS

*I will give them an undivided heart and put a new spirit in them;
I will remove from them their heart of stone and give them a
heart of flesh. Then they will follow my decrees and be careful to
keep my laws. They will be my people and I will be their God. —
Ezekiel 12:19-20 (NIV)*

My Dear Marathoner, please don't forget about the important exchange that took place when you asked Jesus to be your personal Lord and Savior. Ezekiel prophesied about the wonderful time when through Messiah God's people would be able to have the life of God on the inside of them as opposed to the Law on the outside. You've been given an undivided heart and a new spirit. The heartbeat of God Himself is pounding in your chest. You have become one of God's people. Even if my treadmill was fixed by the CEO of the company himself, it could never experience such a transformation. All the self-help books in the world and religious rules and rituals can never do the same job as the life-changing power of the Holy Spirit. He gives you strength, hope, love and joy in a way you've never known before. He has literally placed His power and desires inside of you so you can passionately live out your life to the fullest and glorify Him in all you do.

Week 2: WHEN YOUR TREADMILL BREAKS

Day 7 (Rest Day, Meditation) THE WORK OF RESTORATION

The Lord has anointed me... to bestow on them a crown of beauty instead of ashes, the oil of gladness instead of mourning, and a garment of praise instead of spirit of despair. — Isaiah 61:1a,3b (NIV)

My Dear Marathoner, one day in a devotional is not enough to cover the depth of the beautiful work of restoration God can do in your heart. Today during your meditation time focus on the three things mentioned in the verse above: the crown of beauty, the oil of gladness, and the garment of praise. They symbolize your physical, emotional, and spiritual health. Can you see yourself possessing all three of these things? As you go through your day, ask the Lord to reveal to you the extent to which you could experience them. Ask Jesus to bestow them on you. It will take more than one day to walk through the process of deliverance but you can start today by allowing Him to work in you.

By the way, in case you were wondering, my treadmill got fixed. It took the help of the manufacturer, the diligence of my husband, and guidance from the troubleshooting manual to replace the necessary parts. Now I can take it easy on myself again and avoid running in the elements. I know things don't always come together as easily in real life but they ultimately do work out if we ask God for help.

Here again are the three things to ponder and pray about today:

Ask God for a crown of beauty instead of ashes. God can restore whatever has been destroyed; He removes the spirit of death that has brought spiritual ashes to your life.

Ask God to anoint you with the oil of gladness instead of mourning. God can restore your joy; He removes regrets and comforts you in your our losses.

Ask God to give you a garment of praise instead of spirit of despair. He removes the depression and heaviness from your heart and replaces it with joyful praise and thankfulness.

Week 3: THE DO'S AND DON'TS OF RUNNING

Day 1 (Long Run 10 miles) A DAILY TRAINING MINIMUM?

He has made us competent as ministers of a new covenant — not of the letter but of the Spirit; for the letter kills, but the Spirit gives life. — 2 Corinthians 3:6 (NIV)

As I pointed out in the beginning of this devotional, I am not really planning on giving athletic advice here. There are some common sense truths that apply to our Christian walk just as they apply to running, but only if we apply them in the right way. Please let me explain what I mean by applying them in the *right way.* For example, browsing through some online Christian blogs on running I found a common theme that talked about meeting a daily training requirement. Translated into Christian terms, it meant fulfilling at least a minimum dose of Bible reading and prayer time on a regular basis. So, you didn't read your Bible today. What happens to your training in faith now? Did you mess it up? Do you feel like your coach, a.k.a. God, is now unhappy with you? How about a more realistic scenario? You are a young mom of a preschooler and a toddler and you haven't picked up your Bible in more than a month. (It happened to me, but shhh, don't tell anybody!). All of a sudden you start feeling guilty, not worthy of intimacy with God. You feel like He changed His mind regarding your call to run the race and you got disqualified. I bet this is because you believed a lie that you were supposed to meet some legalistic standard and you fell short. The truth is there is nothing in your abilities or discipline that qualified you in His eyes in the first place.

I agree that if I missed a month of marathon training, getting back on track would be very challenging and put me at risk of injury. My performance in the marathon would almost certainly not be as great as if I had trained consistently. This is where I believe physical and spiritual running differ immensely. Yes, we might have missed out on some great encounters with God when we neglected our times of prayer and Bible reading but if we go after Him with all our hearts He will graciously allow us to make up the lost time. Remember, God is our Father, not an angry coach.

Question to ponder on your long run or throughout the day: Do you carry any sense of guilt that holds you back from getting back on track? Jesus paid the full price on the cross to make up for every time you've fallen short. He calls you to run with Him not because you are a disciplined runner but because He wants you to experience His love.

Week 3: THE DO'S AND DONT'S OF RUNNING

Day 2 (Short Run 4 miles) HYDRATE

As the deer pants for streams of water, so my soul pants for you,
O God. — Psalm 42:1 (NIV)

If I could give you one common sense advice for long distance running, it would be to drink enough water. Not skipping water stations during a marathon pays off. The funny thing about this rule is that it is easy to follow. You will drink water because you will naturally get thirsty. So it is with your spiritual walk. When you first draw near to God you realize how satisfying this experience really is. You understand that He alone can truly satisfy your thirst for self-fulfillment, love, acceptance, and many other things. In the Bible, water often symbolizes the Holy Spirit. It is the Holy Spirit who brings us into the presence of God, who gives us wisdom to understand God's word and who forms our character (fruit) and empowers us to fulfill our calling in life. Just as runners fill up on fluids during a race, the Bible calls us to continuously be filled with the Spirit (Ephesians 5:18b).

Week 3: THE DO'S AND DONT'S OF RUNNING

Day 3 (Rest Day) REST

For the Lord takes delight in his people... — Psalm 149:4a (NIV)

How simple is that – rest on a rest day? It is important that you occasionally pull away from what you are working so hard on. However, it is much easier to make your body stop than your brain! Think of ways to distract yourself by focusing on something that brings you pleasure. Write a note to a friend, plan a vacation, watch sports, go fishing or take a walk. Set aside the anxiety of trying to please by doing things *for* Him. Instead, do something you really enjoy *with* Him. Just think about this – you were created to bring pleasure to God. God takes delight in you! Rest in that thought and enjoy doing things you love together with Him. How does that make your day different?

Week 3: THE DO'S AND DONT'S OF RUNNING

Day 4 (Short Run, Speed Training 4 miles) GAIN MUSCLE

No pain, no gain — An athletic proverb

This is another process that happens naturally. As you continue training, your muscle tissue inevitably increases, becomes stronger, and is able to endure longer repetitive use. When you exercise for the first time, you know you'll be very sore the next day. As I start to run outside after a long season of treadmill running, my legs always get tight for a few days because outside running requires more muscle use than the treadmill does. You can blame this soreness on lactic acid build up. For the muscles to grow, they actually need to break down first, causing you to be sore.

When you commit to taking on some spiritual challenges, you will surely see the same effects. You will have to get over the "soreness" and discomfort in order to press on to the next level. The best thing you can do for your physical muscles when they are sore is to keep moving and stretching. If you try to keep them still, they will become painfully tight. In the same way, you don't want to stop at the first sign of discomfort in your spiritual walk. Later, when we talk about being "in the zone," I will discuss dealing with discomfort a little more.

Week 3: THE DO'S AND DON'TS OF RUNNING

Day 5 (Short Run 4 miles) EAT WELL

Give us today our daily bread. — Matthew 6:11 (NIV)

A vast amount of athletic literature is devoted to proper nutrition. You can find a plethora of often contradicting advice on carbs vs. a high protein diet, every source trying to tackle the issue from a new angle. The bottom line is this: you need to have a healthy and balanced diet to be able to perform well. Let's say you have a choice between a banana and a doughnut before you go on a run. Which one of the two will you go for? We all know what the right answer should be, although I've heard about people who could stop by a bakery on their run, get a doughnut and then keep running. Athletes learn to view food as fuel. Eating is no longer considered as something you do for pleasure: it is something you do to get the right kind of energy. However, when you develop good eating habits, you eventually start to enjoy eating right. What kind of "food" do we eat on our spiritual journey? Do we feed ourselves with movies, commercials, music, and relationships that fill us for a while but then leave us weak and unsatisfied? The Word of God is called the "Bread of Life" for a reason. This is the "carbo-load" that will give us sustainable energy to complete our race successfully.

Week 3: THE DO'S AND DON'TS OF RUNNING

Day 6 (Short Run 4 miles) INCREASE GRADUALLY

Excellence is the gradual result of always striving to do better. —
Pat Riley[6]

Remember, training is a gradual process. They say that if you increase your weekly mileage by more than 10%, you run the risk of injury. Don't worry about running those first 18 miles yet. If you first run 10, then 13, and then 15 you will eventually get up to 18. And I tell you what, after you do your first 18, going back to 13 will feel like nothing!

If you are trying to grow in your faith, start exercising it. Don't expect the first time you have courage to pray for a sick person at the mall that God will make you raise the dead the next day. In the same way, if you give your first offering in obedience to God, it doesn't mean that your business will bring you a fortune a week later. In order to grow in any area, we need to demonstrate a consistent, gradual increase in obedience. Just continue stepping out in faith, even if you start with baby steps at first, and you will see God opening more and more doors for you.

Week 3: THE DO'S AND DON'TS OF RUNNING

Day 7 (Rest Day, Meditation) PUT ONE FOOT IN FRONT OF THE OTHER

But when he asks, he must believe and not doubt, because he who doubts is like a wave of the sea, blown and tossed by the wind. That man should not think he will receive anything from the Lord; he is a double minded man, unstable in all he does. —
James 1:6-8 (NIV)

I am not trying to make fun. This is why I think running is so fascinating. The only thing you're really doing is putting one foot in front of the other, and yet it is as much of a mental process as it is physical! Running truly is a mental exercise. If you can't handle it in your head, you won't be able to in your body. As I am running long distances during this marathon preparation, I am realizing more and more that my mind is learning how to handle a long distance course just as much as my legs are. This is why many times in this devotional I will urge you to engage your mind in the things that are beneficial for boosting your performance. How are you going to get to the finish line? By simply putting one foot ahead of the other, while letting your thoughts and imagination focus on God and His perspective. That way you'll know for sure if you are making progress.

Meditation and prayer:

Do you have double-mindedness about an area in your life? This kind of divided state of mind will make you step from side to side or even backwards instead of going forward. Give this area to the Lord in prayer and get His perspective on it. This will help you to keep pressing forward in your race.

Week 4: FREEDOM TO RUN

Day 1 (Long Run 8 miles) BREAKING FREE

The Lord sets prisoners free. — Psalm 146:7b (NIV)

My Dear Marathoner, just picture yourself watching the beginning of an Olympic race. The crowd is cheering and the announcer is calling the contestants to the starting line. Everything is the way it should be on a day like this except for one thing: the runners are helplessly rolling around on the ground, their bodies tightly bound by ropes. Some of them are eventually able to loosen their ties and try to run, but trip over the cords dangling around their feet. Only those who are able to throw off the ropes completely are able to run and finish the race. What was meant to be a running contest turned out to be a test of whether the runners could break free. Their running ability did not determine the outcome of the race.

What kinds of things inhibit you from running your course smoothly? Right now some of you who are reading this are feeling so tied up you can't take a single step.   Outside circumstances can surely paralyze us, but what is often more binding is how our mind processes our challenges and how we then choose to react in response. The Bible talks about a number of things that intend to rob us of our strength to run and trip us up at the start line. These are the bondages of sin, unforgiveness (not just of others but also of self), fear, and unbelief (or, I should say, belief in the enemy's lies). I might be missing some, but these are the big ones. This week I would like us to honestly assess our hindrances, so we can throw off these ropes and run the way God intended for us to run.

During your day or on your long run ask the Lord to show you the areas in your life where you are experiencing bondage.

Simply ask Him to set you free. He is the only one who can take off the ties. You may not feel any different right away, but you need to trust Him by faith. Renounce the negative ties out loud and declare the truth of God over this area of your life. For example, you might say "I renounce the fear of failure. I declare that God has ordained my steps and has purposed me for success." Complete freedom might seem impossible to you but His word promises "If the Son makes you free, you will be free indeed." (John 8:36, NIV) Don't settle for a life of bondage when "it is for freedom that Christ has set you free." (Galatians 5:1)

Week 4: FREEDOM TO RUN

Day 2 (Short Run 4 miles) RUNNING TO OR RUNNING FROM?

Many people spend their entire lives reacting to what they don't want to be instead of responding to the call of God on their lives.
— *Kris Vallotton, The Supernatural Ways of Royalty*[7]

Very often we get ourselves tied up by running in circles and end up at the same spot we started over and over again. Instead of heading for our goal we dwell in the past. I've heard many people say that they ended up becoming just like the person that hurt them because they spent their life reacting to the hurt instead of learning to forgive. Fear of financial lack is another example of "running from" that drives people to make life choices based on what they have or don't have. In my own life's race I was bound by an intense fear of becoming overweight because in my childhood I witnessed my mother struggling with the same problem. Instead of pursuing a goal of being healthy my mind was constantly obsessed with how much I weighed. Not surprisingly, I always found myself in the same hole - losing a battle with overeating. It took me several years to finally learn to trust and allow God to completely steer me away from that kind of mentality.

Week 4: FREEDOM TO RUN

Day 3 (Rest and Meditation) FORGIVNESS

Seven times, seventy times
I'll do what it takes to make it right.
I thought the pain was here to stay but forgiveness made a way...
— 7×70, Song Lyrics[8]

How do you forgive a rapist, a drunk driver who kills a child, or an unfaithful spouse? The list of terrible offenses can go on and on and the natural way of thinking says you just don't, it's impossible. Yet, the Bible says you will remain in the prison of torment until you do. How can you run the race when you are locked up in jail? You end up behind emotional bars even though the person who trespassed against you might deserve to be behind actual bars by law. The first step to freedom is the hardest – making a decision to let go and forgive. Once you've made up your mind you can pray something like this: "God, I forgive and release ___ (person's name) for what they've done to me. Give me the strength and power to do so. This person is now free from my unforgiveness and I am free." Your feelings may tell you otherwise but you have to trust the truth that Jesus paid the full price on the cross for you to be able to do it. When bitterness tries to haunt you again you need to stand up to it by declaring your freedom. Eventually your feelings will catch to the decision of your will.

Another big part of this topic is the forgiveness of self. Sometimes this is even harder than forgiving someone else. Yet, the Word of God is clear on this issue: Jesus died on the cross to wipe all the sin and shame from your life. He will also give you the power to change and will restore you. My Dear Marathoner, you need to release yourself before God from what you've done.

Meditation and prayer:

Pray that the Holy Spirit shows you if there is anyone you need to forgive. Ask Him to reveal to you the truth of how God sees the situation and the other person, and pray the prayer that I suggested above. As you kneel or stand before God ask Him to minister emotional healing to you.

Think about this verse: "If you, O Lord, kept a record of sins, O Lord, who could stand? But with you there is forgiveness..." (Ps 130:3-4a, NIV)

Week 4: FREEDOM TO RUN

Day 4 (Short Run, Speed Training 4 miles) A NEW STANDARD

> *...Let us throw off everything that hinders and the sin that so easily entangles, and let us run with perseverance the race marked out for us. — Hebrews 12:1b (NIV)*

Can we ever live a sinless life? We can never conform to God's standard of holiness on our own. However, we can take a stand by making a decision to live in line with who He says we are, trusting that God is the One who will empower us to do so. According to Strong's Dictionary, the root word for "sin" in Hebrew is *chata'*.[9] *Chata'* means "to miss, to forfeit." Missing the way and running in the wrong direction in a race would be horrible. Would you really want to forfeit after training so hard? Jesus said "I am the way and the truth and the life" (John 14:6). If we follow Him wholeheartedly we can be assured He will not let us miss the mark. We are told that "there is now no condemnation for those who are in Christ Jesus" in Romans 8:1. God sees us as though we've never sinned through the blood of Christ. When we think of ourselves in that light it is easier to break away from sinful habits and withstand temptation.

Week 4: FREEDOM TO RUN

Day 5 (Short Run 4 miles) MENTALITY OF TRUST

As it is written: "See, I lay in Zion a stone that causes men to stumble and a rock that makes them fall, and the one who trusts in him will never be put to shame." — Romans 9:33 (NIV)

It would stink to trip over a rock during a race. I'd feel embarrassed and hope no one had noticed. The Bible says it happens to us if we don't trust in Him. The flip side of the trust coin is letting go of control. When we trust God for our salvation it means we lay down our self-righteousness. When we trust God for our finances it means we are generous to others. In every situation we have a choice to look for God's direction and solutions and a choice to deal with life based on our own human wisdom and the opinions of others. My Dear Marathoner, giving up control is always hard but it's the only way to run our race without stumbling. You will never be ashamed of your decision to trust Him.

Week 4: FREEDOM TO RUN

Day 6 (Short Run 4 miles) FEARLESS LOVE

There is no fear in love. But perfect love drives out fear... — 1
John 4:18a (NIV)

What are your fears? Some of the biggest ones I've dealt
with were the fear of lack, fear of rejection, and the fear of
something bad happening to my loved ones. I've discovered
that in my own life I experienced fear when there was a lack of
awareness and revelation of the love of my Heavenly Father
toward me. Somehow a lie creeps into our heads that God is
holding out on us and that He is setting us up to fail. As a
result, fear and rebellion begin to grow in the areas of our lives
where we are the most vulnerable. My Dear Marathoner, the
love of your Heavenly Father is overflowing toward you. John
4:18 provides the remedy for our fears. If we receive the depth
of His love, any fear we might have been vulnerable to will be
cast out.

Week 4: FREEDOM TO RUN

Day 7 (Rest Day, Meditation) LET THE HEALING BEGIN

Jesus said, "If you hold to my teaching, you are really my disciples. Then you will know the truth and the truth will set you free." — John 8:31-32 (NIV)

The emotional healing process starts the moment you make a decision to believe God's truth regarding yourself and your circumstances. If certain things you believe about a situation in your life bring you into bondage and prevent you from running freely know that there is always a greater truth regarding that situation. Ask God to reveal His perspective to you. What are some "greater" truths that God revealed to you this week? Your healing process will continue as you consciously commit to standing on those truths by thinking and speaking in line with them.

During your meditation time today list three areas in your life you need God's perspective for. Write down insights from Scripture and your prayer time that refer to those areas. Pray that God will fill these areas with His love.

1.
2.
3.

Week 5: BEING IN THE "ZONE"

Day 1 *(Long Run 13 miles)* DETERMINE YOUR "ZONE"

Jesus watched to see where the Father was at work and joined Him... Watch to see where God is working and join Him! — Henry T. Blackaby & Claude V. King, Experiencing God. Knowing and Doing the Will of God[10]

An athlete "in the zone" successfully performs to his or her maximum potential. It is a combination of full involvement, concentration, and energy that brings about enjoyment and satisfaction. When I run long distance, my "in the zone" times usually happen when I run at just the right pace, one I am able to sustain for long periods of time while enjoying myself. How do I get there? Through consistent focused training which gives me confidence and helps me learn how I feel at various paces. Ironically, sometimes it's only a good night's sleep that makes a difference between being "in the zone" and being out of it. As I continue to train and get in better shape, my "zone" thresholds also change.

Apart from running, we all have moments when we feel like we are "in the zone," but more often it feels like we are swimming against a current. I think I can do all these wonderful things, but when push comes to shove I find myself feeling like I don't have enough time, resources, or energy. Jesus said that apart from Him we can do nothing (John 15:5). On one of the occasions after He healed a man on the Sabbath Jesus made a statement that He did only what He saw His Father doing (John 5:19). My Dear Marathoner, don't you think if we were more in tune with the Father, things would flow easier? The best part of it, in my opinion, is that we'd no longer waste our time and energy on things that don't matter.

During the day or on your long run meditate on this Scripture: "For the Father loves the Son and shows him all he does…" (John 5:20a, NIV). This is the hidden key to the door through which we get into the zone in our everyday lives: partnering with God in what He reveals to us.

Week 5: BEING IN THE "ZONE"

Day 2 (Short Run 3 miles) GUIDED BY HIS VOICE

My sheep listen to my voice; I know them, and they follow me. — John 10:27 (NIV)

How do we hear the voice of God? The Bible talks about it as a still, small voice or a gentle whisper (1 Kings 19:12). We learn to recognize it by experience. It's just like in the times before caller ID when you would learn to recognize someone's voice on the phone. If you talked to a person frequently you'd immediately recognize them when they called. The easiest time to hear God is when you are reading the Bible and praying. Make sure you converse with Him and listen. Very often His voice comes in the form of an intense thought or a visual picture that stirs you on the inside while bringing a sense of peace at the same time. Then you can know with great confidence that He is speaking to you. He will always confirm the word He is giving you through Scripture and possibly through another person or outside circumstances as well.

Week 5: BEING IN THE "ZONE"

Day 3 (Rest Day, Meditation) UNDERSTANDING THE WILL OF GOD

Be joyful always; pray continually; give thanks in all circumstances, for this is God's will for you in Christ Jesus. — 1 Thessalonians 5:16-18 (NIV)

When you sign up for a race you can always find a description of its course and view the map on the race's website. They tell you where it starts, what streets are along the route, and what kind of elevation to expect. Don't you wish we had something like that regarding the will of God in our lives? We are given a course description and a map, which is called the Word of God, but sometimes life seems too complicated to apply it in specific situations. The truth is we are not always certain what kind of turn life is going to take. We do have a disclaimer in the Word of God that there will be elevations and uphill battles, troubles and sorrows. We also have great promises that He will make all things work out for our good and that He will never leave us nor forsake us. We can bring Him glory in ALL our circumstances.

I believe part of the reason God doesn't reveal His full plan to us right away is so that we remain dependent on Him every step of the way. He wants to be a part of our daily lives. He wants us to reach out to Him in faith, to seek Him and to inquire of Him. He wants our true identity to be developed in the process. We can be sure of one thing - He will always be faithful to lead us if we agree to follow. As the verse above states, whatever situation we find ourselves in, it is God's will for us to be thankful, to have joy and to continue talking with Him.

Meditation and prayer:

Think about your circumstances right now. What are the things you can give thanks for? Make a mental or a written list and thank Him out loud. My prayer today is "Father, I pray my spirit would always be sensitive to Your guidance. Thank you for everything You are doing in my life."

Week 5: BEING IN THE "ZONE"

Day 4 (Short Run, Speed Training 4 miles) FEELING GOD'S HEARTBEAT

My heart is stirred by a noble theme as I recite my verses for the king; my tongue is the pen of a skillful writer. — Psalm 45:1 (NIV)

The faster you run, the faster your heart beats, and the easier it is to feel its rhythm in your chest. When you are in the midst of a trial or a challenge you may feel like you are accelerating so much that you are almost sprinting. Those challenges cause your life's pulse to rise. And yet, there is another steady, constant, and resounding heartbeat inside of your spirit. It is the heart of God that has been beating inside of you since the day you asked Jesus to be your Savior. When you focus on it and listen to it closely your own heart will be transformed. It will start beating in sync with His. You will see things how He sees them, you will feel His love and compassion toward others and you will become aware of an awesome power that is within you. My Dear Marathoner, stir your heartbeat by a good and "noble theme" and give Him glory and praise!

Week 5: BEING IN THE "ZONE"

Day 5 (Short Run 5 miles) GOD AT WORK

Your will be done on earth as it is in heaven. — Matthew 6:10
(NIV)

God is working in us and around us to bring heaven's will and reality to earth. Joining Him in His work strips us of self-centeredness. My Dear Marathoner, the first and most important part is allowing Him to work in you. You simply can't skip this step: you need to let the Holy Spirit transform you into His dwelling place. God wants to sanctify every room, every area in the "house" so that His heavenly reality becomes evident in your daily life. He wants you to become aware of all the riches He has placed at your disposal and the abundance of His love. This is the kind of reality you need to share when you join Him in His work toward others.

Week 5: BEING IN THE "ZONE"

Day 6 (Short Run 4 miles) OBEDIENCE

To obey is better than sacrifice... — 1 Samuel 15:22 (NIV)

Obedience is not a favorite word for any child. My kids like to be goofy and sometimes get carried away; to them having to obey in those situations seems like giving up their fun. This probably is not your favorite topic either. Why? We obey road signs when we drive because we don't want to get a ticket or worse, die in an accident. We follow rules of dental hygiene because we don't want to get cavities. We often associate lack of obedience with punishment and unwanted circumstances, so our whole concept therefore carries a negative connotation because of our fear of consequences.

Yet, the primary purpose of obedience to God is not to teach us about boundaries and avoiding punishment. I believe that through obedience to God's word we discover how much power it really holds. When we listen to God, it unveils a whole new realm of deep and relevant revelation of Him in our lives. We actually discover that God does not establish a cap on how much of Him we can experience because He desires to mold us into supernatural runners. There is no limit to His love; there is no ceiling to what He can do in and through our lives. Our obedience opens the door for God to manifest Himself; it gives us an opportunity to get closer to fulfilling His call on our lives.

Week 5: BEING IN THE "ZONE"

Day 7 (Rest Day, Meditation) WHAT IF I MISS IT?

I know, O Lord, that a man's life is not his own; it is not for man to direct his steps. — Jeremiah 10:23 (NIV)

What if in a race you didn't notice the orange cones that told you to turn and kept going straight? Hopefully, you would realize what happened soon enough and turn around. You'd be more tired after running those unnecessary miles and would lose some time but you could still finish the race. Fortunately for us, God's race doesn't look exactly the same as a physical course. You can take a deep breath and relax. He does not expect us to get it right every time. In fact, I believe He purposefully allows us to miss it sometimes so He can reveal his redemptive power over the situation. He is sovereign and does not give up on us just because we failed to recognize His will. He looks beyond our words and actions into our heart. We please Him because we are His children and because our hearts are set on following Him, not because we do something right. As a parent myself, I understand this concept very well. I might redirect my children but I will never stop loving them.

Meditation and payer:

Is there a particular situation that comes to your mind where you feel like you missed the "orange cones?" Give that situation to God in prayer and ask Him to release you from guilt and help you see His redemptive work regarding that situation.

Week 6: RUNNING INTO FATHER'S ARMS

Day 1 (Long Run 10 miles) FATHER'S LOVE

Which of you, if his son asks for bread, will give him a stone? Or if he asks for a fish, will give him a snake? If you, then, though you are evil, know how to give good gifts to your children, how much more will your Father in heaven give good gifts to those who ask Him! — Matthew 7:9-11(NIV)

This, perhaps, is the most foundational chapter in the whole devotional. My Dear Marathoner, I really want these seven days to sink deep down into your mind and spirit. What I offer here is much more than psychoanalysis. It truly has the power to transform you for the rest of your life.

What kind of father did you have growing up? What memories do you associate with your earthly dad? Not many can boast that they've had a close emotional bond with their father. Far too many people I've met have hurtful and unresolved issues regarding the father figure in their lives. Even the best fathers are not perfect (and we can never expect them to be) but our Heavenly Father is. The problem is we unconsciously project the image of our earthly fathers onto the image of Father God. We relate to our Heavenly Father mentally and emotionally in similar ways to how we see our earthly father figures unless we receive a revelation of the depth of the Father's Love.

It blows my mind, but here is the truth: the God of the Universe who created the stars, our planet, all the wonderful things of nature and our miraculous bodies with all their intricate cells and systems loves us so much that He wants to have a relationship with us. He wants to be closer to you than your own skin. He put the price tag on your life that equaled the crucifixion of His Son Jesus. He wants you to know that you are His and His Father's heart is filled with love towards you. His eyes are always on you. I was fortunate to have a good earthly father. He knew how to provide and give "good gifts," whether it was a piece of candy that he would bring back from a business trip, or the "gift" of strong character and integrity that he displayed or his value of education and hard work that he instilled in me. But even then, he couldn't always be there. Once I grew up and went my own way, our relationship physically became long distant. I had to realize that, in contrast, my Heavenly Father has never been away, busy, or distant. My Dear Marathoner, during your long run today or just throughout the day meditate on Isaiah 49:15-16 (NIV): Can a mother forget the baby at her breast and have no compassion on the child she has borne? Though she may forget, I will not forget you! See, I have engraved you on the palms of my hands..." I pray reading through this week's devotional will help restore the true image of your Heavenly Father in your mind and heart.

Week 6: RUNNING INTO FATHER'S ARMS

Day 2 (Short Run 4 miles) RUN TO THE FATHER

But while he was still a long way off, his father saw him and was filled with compassion for him; he ran to his son, threw his arms around him and kissed him. — Luke 15:20 (NIV)

The story of the prodigal son shows our Father's heart: it is full of compassion; it makes Father run toward you when He sees you approaching Him. He desires to give you a hug and a kiss, the most intimate expression of family relationships. Whether you are a prodigal or not, this is how He feels about you. So run toward Him! You have nothing to be afraid of. Let your race take you deep into the Father's heart. This is where I am headed. An ultra marathon will feel like a Hawaiian vacation when you are abiding in the secret place of His love. You can run your race while sitting on His lap.

Week 6: RUNNING INTO FATHER'S ARMS

Day 3 (Rest Day, Meditation) FATHER'S IMAGE

I will not leave you as orphans; I will come to you. — *John 14:18*

My Dear Marathoner, spend this day writing out and meditating on the qualities of Father God you can find in the Bible. I can make a pretty long list just off the top of my head. He is our provider, our defender, our healer, our friend and the lover of our souls. He is caring, just, compassionate and patient. He is all powerful, mighty and sovereign. He is faithful. He doesn't change, doesn't lie, doesn't reject, and doesn't fail you or ever forget about you. The world around us tries to distort the image of the Father in our minds. When we embrace false images of our Heavenly Father, then our own image of who God created us to be becomes warped as well. Ask the Holy Spirit to help you identify the lies about Him and yourself that have been planted in your mind. Find a place where you can be alone and pray out loud. Renounce those lies and declare the truths and scriptures that relate to those truths. Here are some examples:

I cast down the lie that told me that I am unattractive. I declare that I am beautiful. God created me and I am "fearfully and wonderfully made." (Psalm 139:14) Father, I accept Your love in this area of my life.

I cast down the lie that told me that I am shameful. I declare that I am free from shame and God is proud of me because I am His son/daughter. Father, I accept Your love in this area of my life.

Please do not be restricted by these examples. Be specific and confident in your declaration of truth. This is not just some self-help exercise. Through your faith and prophetic confession God releases freedom and restores your identity to the way He intended it to be.

Week 6: RUNNING INTO FATHER'S ARMS

Day 4 (Short Run, Speed Training 4 miles) INTIMACY IN FATHER'S ARMS

Better is one day in your courts than a thousand elsewhere... —
Psalm 84:10a (NIV)

Several years ago I was at a conference that featured some truly inspiring speakers on faith. It seemed to me like those men and women were already living in the "promised land" by traveling and speaking all over the world. During one of the sessions my mind drifted and I started asking God about when my time would come to be a missionary and travel to different places. His answer came very clear: "Right now I just want you to travel into My heart, into My presence."

We can't just mentally learn about who we are in God's eyes. Deep understanding of our Father's heart and our own identity can only be imparted when we spend intimate time with Him. We come into His courts through the Holy Spirit by surrendering our lives to Him and conversing with Him just the way we are, without withholding or hiding any of our thoughts and feelings from Him.

My "speed training" challenge to you is to run into Father's arms today and let Him embrace you. Allow yourself to be fully transparent before Him.

Week 6: RUNNING INTO FATHER'S ARMS

Day 5 (Short Run 4 miles) FROM ORPHANS TO SONS

A father to the fatherless... — Psalm 68:5a (NIV)

We have been redeemed and adopted by our Heavenly Father. We have been brought into His family and into His house. So why do we continue to think and act like orphans, not willing to give up our independent "survival" mode of life?

My Dear Marathoner, if you did my "speed challenge" yesterday, this "run" should be very easy. During your intimate time with God let Him impart to you that you are not an orphan. An orphan thinks and acts as if he has no defender or provider; he has no place to go for intimacy and affection. On the contrary, you are a dearly loved son or daughter with a Father who first and foremost values a close relationship with you and cares deeply about your well-being. An orphan has no inheritance. A son or daughter of God has been entrusted with the riches of God's Kingdom. An orphan may not know his or her genetics and family history. God's children have their Father's spiritual DNA implanted in them as a deposit of the Holy Spirit. They know they've been born into the family of a victorious Champion along with many other brothers and sisters.

Week 6: RUNNING INTO FATHER'S ARMS

Day 6 (Short Run 4 miles) NAMED BY THE FATHER

Before I was born the Lord called me; from my birth he has made mention of my name. — Isaiah 49:1b (NIV)

God knew you were going to be born before your parents did. The Bible tells us He knew you from your mother's womb. Your parents put your name on the birth certificate. Yet, the verse above indicates that God was the one who gave you a name that is supposed to define your calling and identity. In my family my dad called me Allochka. It sounds funny in English but in Russian the changed ending of my name means "the dear or precious one." In the intimacy of my family I was called differently than what my friends, teachers, or other people called me. In the intimacy of your Father's house, He may also call you by a special name. Take the time to listen and you will hear it. Here are a few particular names God calls us by in the Bible: children, beloved, saints, friends, disciples, bride, His temple and the apple of His eye. I pray that at least one of them will stand out to you today in a revelatory way and transform your relationship with your Father.

Week 6: RUNNING INTO FATHER'S ARMS

Day 7 (Rest Day, Meditation) LOVE NEVER FAILS

Love never fails. But where there are prophecies, they will cease; where there are tongues, they will be stilled; where there is knowledge, it will pass away... And now these three remain: faith, hope, and love. But the greatest of these is love. — 1 Corinthians 13:8, 13.

You are in a very long race. Once it is all said and done, not much is left at the end of it. The verse above warns you that many things you might rely on right now will pass away, or should I say "pass out," like a runner bonks in a race before getting to the finish line. There will be a time when your education, achievements and material possessions won't matter because they aren't eternal and weren't meant for a long spiritual race. There is one guarantee – love will never pass out, bonk, quit or fail you. People, their promises, your goals and dreams, your health and your circumstances will change. God wants you to know there is one constant you can always rely on during your race – His love. On your end, you might do all these wonderful things during your race but the most valuable thing that will remain at the end is your love toward Him and others. We will talk more about faith, hope, and love again later in our training.

Meditation and prayer:

Try to honestly assess your choices, decisions and actions of the past week. How many of these choices, decisions and actions were driven by, inspired by or rooted in your love toward others and toward God? Ask God in prayer to saturate you with His love. Pray that He will give you opportunities to show His love to others through you.

Week 7: WHAT IF I FALL?

Day 1 (Long Run 15 miles) IT HAPPENS TO THE BEST OF US

http://www.youtube.com/watch?v=768IV_WO4ec [11]

http://www.youtube.com/watch?v=kZlXWp6vFdE [12]

My Dear Marathoner, instead of starting this day with a quote, watch these two moving Youtube clips and see if you don't shed some tears over them like I did. The first link shows the 600m race at the Big 10 Indoor Track Championships in 2008. University of Minnesota runner Heather Dorniden tripped and crashed in the last 200 meters only to get up and catch up to her opponents who had been far gone. As the author of the post put it, that race was "not about a fall," but "about a rise." And it was quite a breathtaking rise. The second link features Derek Redmond at the 1992 Olympics in Barcelona. Redmond was favored to become a medalist in the 400 meter sprint but 150 meters into the race he tore his hamstring. He rejected medical help and continued limping on one foot toward the finish line. Watch and cry as I did as you see Redmond's father breaking through security and embracing his son. Redmond and his father walked the rest of the distance together, Derek leaning on his father's shoulder. Right before the end, Derek's father let him go to cross the finish line on his own. The author of the post concludes it with the phrase: "When you don't give up, you can't fail."

It is important to remember in the middle of our struggles that God has purposed us for success. He has a victorious ending in mind for us and He never sets us up for failure. However, we all make mistakes and failures happen to the best of us. In fact, if we knew we couldn't fail, then we would never try hard at anything and would never attempt to reach our greatest potential because we would take our success for granted. Failures are meant to make us better. They also reveal our true character and determination (or the lack of it). They are the best times to connect with God and allow Him to show us the bigger picture and transform us through our failure experience. He wants to walk with us like Derek Redmond's father, so we can make it to the finish line and cross it.

During your long run or throughout your day think about your most recent failure. How did it affect you and the people around you? Have you noticed any changes in yourself or your decisions because of that? Have you ever allowed God to work through this experience with you?

Week 7: WHAT IF I FALL?

Day 2 (Short Run 3 miles) WILL TO GET BACK UP

I literally thought that I just skinned my knees and put my hands down and got back up. I never realized I skidded on my stomach on the ground. I was bouncing on the track. — Heather Dorniden[13]

In the heat of a race when your whole being is set on one goal and years of training are bursting through every cell of your body you don't have time to decide whether you want to get back up or not. You just do it without noticing the real damage until after the race is over.

Your God is greater than any failure or disappointment you might experience. If you are possessed by His vision for your life its driving force will help lift you back up on your feet and you will continue charging toward the finish line. Your solid faith training in God's Word will provide the strength you need to get up and make your race count.

Week 7: WHAT IF I FALL?

Day 3 (Rest Day, Meditation) LOOKING PAST THE HURT AND EMBARRASMENT

And we know that in all things God works for the good of those who love him, who have been called according to his purpose. —
Romans 8:28 (NIV)

The devil will try to make sure you feel hurt and embarrassment in the moment of your fall. If you take the time to discuss the issue with him in the aftermath you will find it harder to move on. His whole purpose is to knock you out of the race. If you continue listening to him regarding your past failures, it will be like running while constantly looking over your shoulder or driving while looking in the rearview mirror. That's a great way to trip again or to have an even worse accident.

Meditation and prayer:

During your meditation time today, ask God to expose the voice of the enemy that you might have listened to. The most obvious signs of this voice are the thoughts that contradict God's word and promote hopelessness, self-pity and a lack of self-worth. These thoughts cause feelings of helplessness, anger, jealousy, bitterness and hatred. Make up your mind not to give in to the voice of the devil and tune in to God's voice that will show you how to look past your failures and falls and move on with His abundant grace and power.

Week 7: WHAT IF I FALL?

Day 4 (Short Run, Speed Training 5 miles) KICKING INTO A HIGHER GEAR

It's probably one of my greatest running memories of all time. It's something that is completely unexplainable to me besides through a higher power. I feel like the Lord just filled me up and gave me the opportunity to show what amazing things can happen through Him. — Heather Dorniden[14]

When talking about what happened to her after the fall, Heather Dorniden said it felt to her like she kicked into a higher gear she did not realize she had before. This is what God's grace and forgiveness does to you after you decide to repent, believe Him and continue on His path. It takes you to a gear you never knew existed. Suddenly you realize the changes and transformation God is bringing forth through your failure experience. One of the greatest examples of this I've seen is in His work of marriage restoration. In my own marriage every conflict my husband and I submitted to the Lord and each other resulted in greater closeness and refreshing in our relationship. I've seen other friends' marriages restored and broken hearts renewed by the Lord. I've witnessed people coming out of drug and alcohol addictions and living productive lives because of the redemptive power of Christ.

As a speed challenge for today, allow God to take you up a notch. Ask for deliverance from any sin in your life that might have caused you to fall. Accept His spiritual, emotional and physical restoration.

Week 7: WHAT IF I FALL?

Day 5 (Short Run 5 miles) BURSTING PAST YOUR OPPONENTS

*For our struggle is not against flesh and blood, but
against the authorities, against the powers of this dark world
and against the spiritual forces of evil in the heavenly realms.* —
Ephesians 6:12 (NIV)

Your opponents are not human. It may be hard to believe in a spiritual reality in our day and age but the Bible is very clear on its existence and its effect on the human race. You are not competing against anyone you know and you are not fighting against anyone who might have done you wrong. What you really need to outrun and defeat are the spiritual forces of fear, insecurity and destructive sinful behaviors. When you fall it might seem like those nasty things have several laps on you. If you walk in unbelief and lack of awareness of your spiritual power in Christ you will stay defeated, lying on the track instead of rising up to overcome the enemy of your soul. God wants to bring you into a place where by His grace and power you burst into a sprint that causes you to leave your opponents in the dust. As a child of God you have the blood of Christ that protects you and ensures your victory over every spiritual force of evil. Learn to recognize it and run with the authority He's given you.

Week 7: WHAT IF I FALL?

Day 6 (Short Run 4 miles) SEIZING YOUR OPPORTUNITY

In the middle of difficulty lies opportunity. — Albert Einstein[15]

Sometimes I wonder if I would have picked up running if I were naturally thin and didn't struggle with gaining extra weight. The answer is probably not. Yet, having to always watch my weight turned out to be a blessing in disguise. It caused me to exercise. I still remember the sunny spring morning my husband and I came out for our first run. I was fed up with my sedentary life style of writing grad school papers all day long. It was time to get active. The half-mile loop in the park could have been a novice-friendly course if not for a long steep hill at the end. My husband made it to the top but I didn't. Out of breath and with legs feeling like jelly I watched him finish from the middle of the hill. That was my first run. It ended in what seemed like a failure. Little did I know that six months later I would run my first marathon. It all started with an attempt to overcome my struggle with extra weight and determination to finally conquer that dreadful hill. Very shortly my exercise turned into a game of how long I could run and how many times I could scale that hill in one workout. I ended up falling in love with long distance running without even noticing.

My Dear Marathoner, ask God to show you the opportunities that lie in the middle of your hardship and failure. They are like secret treasures hidden in a heap of trash. Carefully sort out the good from the bad. Discard the trash and use the treasures. Even if you can't see those treasures, God can. He sees potential for strengthening your faith in every kind of circumstance.

Week 7: WHAT IF I FALL?

Day 7 (Rest Day, Meditation) FINISHING IN VICTORY

You raise me up, so I can stand on mountains,
You raise me up to walk on stormy seas;
I am strong when I am on your shoulders,
You raise me up to more than I can be.
— *You Raise Me Up, Song Lyrics*[16]

Sometimes it is not the gold medal that brings you fame. It is your ability to handle adversity that gives you a more meaningful victory than a medal. When you give God your hand, He lifts you up. As I am writing this, I am suddenly overtaken by a forgotten childhood memory. When I was little, my dad used to take me with him to the Labor Day Parade that was held in Russia every year on May 1st. The parade was held in every city in the country and it was a big deal. The whole community was part of it and it was shown on TV. People walked in columns, holding banners and waving flags representing various organizations, work places and schools. To me as a child the parade was not about making any dogmatic statements or propaganda forced by the government. It was about proudly riding on my dad's shoulders as he led his school ahead of the float. On my dad's shoulders I felt like I could see everything and everyone could see me, maybe even on TV. I felt like I was on top of the world.

Your heavenly Daddy is leading the parade. No matter how low you've fallen, if you repent and come back to Him, you will be on top of the world when you ride on His shoulders. Everybody sees His glory and you become part of it.

As part of your meditation today, ask God to raise you up to more than you can ever be. Picture yourself riding on His shoulders. How does it feel?

Week 8: WHAT'S YOUR TERRAIN?

Day 1 (Long Run 12 miles) NO MOUNTAIN HIGH, NO VALLEY LOW

Neither height nor depth, nor anything else in all creation, will be able to separate us from the love of God that is in Christ Jesus our Lord. — Romans 8:39 (NIV)

If you are a runner in Pennsylvania you know there are very few places for running that are flat, especially in Pittsburgh, where my in-laws live. I always return home with sore glutes and calves after jogging in their neighborhood. I can relate to the people of Israel who constantly travelled and lived in the midst of mountains and valleys. Both mountains and valleys are symbolic of challenges we face in our life's journey. Mountains are hard to ascend and the valleys are tough because they are so low you can't see where the path ultimately leads to. Through their wanderings, the nation of Israel became conditioned for the uneven terrain of their spiritual journey. Our life experiences can be like mountains and valleys and God wants to condition our faith so we can handle both.

I picked my first two marathons based on the fact that they were flat. Not a bad idea for a beginner. Now, this one in Pittsburgh will be different. We'll see how I can handle those hills. In life, we don't get to choose our terrain. What is it like for you right now? My Dear Marathoner, no matter whether you are climbing a steep mountain or heading down into a dark valley, know that on top of every mountain you can have an encounter with God and every valley can be filled by His presence. I am writing this to myself because I know I am venturing into a terrain filled with new valleys and mountains. Just a few days ago I was faced with the fact that my little daughter's leg bones are not growing properly. I know I may be entering a season of challenging questions, deep concerns, possible surgeries, difficult physical therapy and burdensome financial expenses. Before it is all said and done, this book will be finished and you may never know how it all ends but I have to assure you and myself that God will be with us through every mountain and every valley. I choose to trust in God's love and His supernatural ability to heal.

Week 8: WHAT'S YOUR TERRAIN?

Day 2 (Short Run 4 miles) LIKE THE FEET OF A DEER

The Sovereign Lord is my strength; he makes my feet like the feet of a deer, he enables me to tread on the heights. — *Habakkuk 3:19*

In my early college years when I still lived in Russia I used to hike with friends at a place in Siberia that had several huge rock formations called "pillars." Some of them were dangerous to climb without special rock climbing equipment but others had enough ledges and footholds for a person to get to the top if they knew what they were doing. I was not one of those rock climbing experts but every time I stood at the foot of the "pillars" they beckoned me. I would climb about ten feet and feel like going higher and higher. One time I actually followed a friend who had some climbing experience and made it to the very top! The thrill of conquering a 250 foot rock and the breathtaking bird's-eye view made me forget about the risk I had just taken. I am not sure if deer would climb a rock like that but I can imagine how amazing it would be to have a mountain animal's strong and well balanced feet that could gracefully leap on the rocks and scale the mountains. That's exactly what God promises to us when we are faced with mountains in our lives. He gives us the strength and agility to scale the heights as if we were naturals at it. Just as my friend did, He will show you the right ledges and footholds to step on, so you can safely conquer any peak.

Week 8: WHAT'S YOUR TERRAIN?

Day 3 (Rest Day, Meditation) KILLER HILL, IS IT WORTH IT?

The higher the mountain, the harder the climb, the better the view from the top. — Anonymous[17]

"Test your will on Orchard Hill," — says a slogan on my long sleeve tee that I got for running the Nittany Valley Half Marathon a few months ago. Somebody posted on the race website that the hill made you "see God." And I agree; it was quite a killer hill. What made it especially hard in a physical sense was that it was very long and it came at the very end of the race when I didn't have much strength left. However, I believe that hill was even tougher to take mentally. On my way to the top, I noticed that the course elevation itself was not very steep but the road was surrounded by almost vertical hills on every side. If I looked at those hills while running it seemed like my own path was much steeper than it really was. I purposefully refused to look around and kept my eyes just a few steps ahead of me.

My Dear Marathoner, the hills around that course are like the "what ifs" of our lives. When we look at those mountains we listen to our fears and regrets. We exhaust our mental and emotional strength thinking about climbing them even though we don't have to. Instead, God calls us to run the elevation that He knows we can handle. We need to look at Him and the promises He has for us, not the mountains on either side. Once we are at the top, the view will be magnificent.

Meditation and payer:

Are you wasting your mental energy on what exhausts you instead of on what helps you to achieve your goals? Ask God to refocus your eyes on what matters.

Week 8: WHAT'S YOUR TERRAIN?

Day 4 (Short Run, Speed Training 4 miles)
CONDITIONED FOR HILLS

How beautiful on the mountains are the feet of those who bring
good news. — Isaiah 52:7 (NIV)

My Dear Marathoner, my challenge for today's speed training is for you to look for someone to encourage. Giving a simple compliment to someone or wishing someone a nice day might be all it takes. At other times, it might require dropping your personal plans and spending hours with someone just listening to them talk about their troubles. You can always share the good news of the Gospel that Jesus brings forgiveness, salvation and hope with people who need encouragement. You are conditioned to bring this kind of message to the ones around you and help them through their mountain climbs.

Week 8: WHAT'S YOUR TERRAIN?

Day 5 (Short Run 4 miles) MOUNTAINS AND VALLEYS INSIDE OF US

Every valley shall be filled in, every mountain and hill made low. The crooked roads shall become straight, the rough ways smooth. — Luke 3:5 (NIV)

We are called to prepare a straight path and a smooth terrain in our own hearts for God to operate in the fullness of His glory. It is impossible without grasping the concept of grace. Jesus died on the cross for our sin. Because He was the only one without sin He was able to conquer death and rise to life. As much as we try, we can never earn God's salvation or add to what He has already accomplished. Our self-righteous attempts to earn His favor act like mountains inside of our souls that stand in the way of God's work in us. We need to accept the fact that all He does in us is because of His grace and is not based on our own merit. He is also the One who will fill every void in our souls like a river that floods an empty valley. We try to fill the emptiness inside with many different things such as relationships, money, food, alcohol or exercise, forgetting that He is the only One who can really satisfy. No wonder our paths are crooked and rough when we put other things ahead of God. But He can straighten and smooth out every uneven terrain. We just need to yield to the work of His Spirit by admitting that we can't fulfill our life's purpose on our own and by asking Him to saturate us and to move in us and through us.

Week 8: WHAT'S YOUR TERRAIN?

Day 6 (Short Run 4 miles) PLACES OF REVELATION

That is the nature of revelation – it opens up new realms of living, of possibility, of faith. — *Bill Johnson, The Supernatural Power of a Transformed Mind*[18]

Mountain top experiences can be quite revelatory. Not many respond to the challenge of a steep mountain hike, so mountain peaks are solitary places. There are no distractions, just you and God. That's where He reveals to you His heart and His purposes. The word revelation in Greek is *apokalypsis*[19] and it means "to be revealed, to lighten, manifestation, coming, appearing." Just like faith, revelation is more than head knowledge. It is an experience within your spirit when certain concepts you've mentally known before become so real they change you on the inside.

How do you reach a mountain top experience with God? It might seem like you have to jump through hoops and pass some kind of test in order to get into His presence. However, in reality, there is no step-by-step formula. It is the Holy Spirit who takes you there. All you need to do is to pursue it by faith and ask the Holy Spirit to take you right up to the Throne Room. Spending time in worship when you exalt God to His proper place will help you create an atmosphere of hunger for Him that will draw His presence. Follow His lead. He might overwhelm you with an intense feeling of His love or highlight scripture in your mind that will suddenly pop up in your thoughts like a 3-D image and become meaningful and relevant. He might give you a song to worship with, an inspiration to write or a solution to your problem. No matter what God reveals to you on your mountain top or what way He does it, He will stir up your spirit to desire Him more and more.

Week 8: WHAT'S YOUR TERRAIN?

Day 7 (Rest Day, Meditation) THE VIEW FROM THE TOP

Call to me, and I will answer you, and show you great and mighty things, which you do not know. — Jeremiah 33:3 (NKJV)

In this country a good view is worth a lot. People are willing to pay money in order to enjoy beautiful scenery. Properties that have a nice view cost more than the ones that don't. I like running races that go past picturesque sites. I ran my first marathon in Virginia Beach where you stare at the ocean waves from the Bay Bridge for the first half of the race. An ocean view was more than enough to inspire me for a long run. My second was the Marine Corps Marathon in Washington, DC. That was a different kind of setting that offered a variety of mind-capturing historical scenery during the run. I expect to see some panoramic sights from the bridges in Pittsburgh also.

Nothing beats a view from the top of a mountain. God always has a bigger picture. He knows things we don't. He is willing to share His perspective with us; that's why He is drawing us up to those mountain peaks. He wants us to be able to see things how He sees them. You can stand at the peak with Him and say "Wow, what a magnificent view!" Some mountain tops go even higher than the clouds where the sun is always shining. It can be cloudy and overcast down at the foot of the mountain but you know the sun is still there above the clouds. But what happens when we go down to the valley again? Do we forget the view we've just seen? I believe God wants us to live in the valley by relying on the reality that we've seen from the top of the mountain. We can't see it from below but it is still there. We can't abide at the top of the mountain forever but we can always carry in our hearts the truth we've seen from the top.

During your meditation time today ask God to remind you of the views you've seen during your mountain top experiences with Him. And if you can't think of one, don't get discouraged. Just ask Him to take you there.

Week 9: A RELAY RACE

DAY 1 (Long Run 18 miles) THE FIRST RELAY LEG

I tell you the truth, anyone who has faith in me will do what I have been doing. He will do even greater things than these, because I am going to the Father. — John 14:12 (NIV)

I don't know if you have figured this out yet, but you are in a faith relay race. Jesus actually started it and ran the first leg. Have you ever seen a relay race where the first runner so dominates the other contestants that no matter how the rest of his teammates do, their team is so far ahead after the first leg that they are guaranteed a win? This is what Jesus did for us. He secured the victory in this race with His blood. He taught the world about the Father and the meaning of true love and then He said, "Go into all the world and preach the good news to all creation." (Mark 16:15) Will you agree to be on His team, to take the baton and pass it on? This is the choice the first disciples had to make when He looked them in the eye and said, "Go and make disciples of all the nations..." (Matthew 28:19) If you were there would you have taken the baton from Him, knowing the price of suffering and persecution you'd have to pay?

What did the baton look like when Jesus passed it along? Right before He told His disciples to go into all the world, He said, "All authority in heaven and on earth has been given to Me..." (Matthew 28:18) The Gospel of Mark elaborates on this authority by listing the signs that will accompany those who take the baton of faith: they will drive out demons in His name, they will speak in new tongues, they will not be hurt by snakes, if they drink deadly poison it will not harm them and they will place their hands on sick people and they will get well (Mark 16:17-18). The Gospel of Luke says the baton was given to the disciples along with the promise to be "clothed with power from on high" (Luke 24:49) which came to pass on the day of Pentecost.

The baton that Jesus passed along was charged with high spiritual voltage. It wasn't supposed to lose its power over the years and it hasn't. When you apply faith to the word of God your baton is just as powerful as it was when it came right from the hands of Jesus to the first disciples. Now that I have described it to you in this way, will you still agree to take it?

During your day or your long run mediate on how running with the baton of Jesus would affect your life and the lives of those around you. Run with all your heart; you know you will not fail because Jesus is on your team!

Week 9: A RELAY RACE

Day 2 (Short Run 3 miles) PART OF A TEAM

Now the body is not made up of one part but many... You are the body of Christ, and each one of you is a part of it. — 1 Corinthians 12:14, 27 (NIV)

My Dear Marathoner, welcome to the team! I hope you feel like a part of a family. I've actually never ran a real relay race but I can imagine that I would try even harder if I knew that others were dependent on my results. I wouldn't want to let my team down. What if I just decided not to show up for my leg of the race? My absence would create a huge void for my team. One of my teammates would have to run double the distance to make up for my carelessness, or worse, the team could get disqualified. There is a level of responsibility that comes with being a team member. You just can't live only by what feels right for you. You have to consider the effect that you have on others, including the generations to come.

Week 9: A RELAY RACE

Day 3 (Rest Day, Meditation) FROM GENERATION TO GENERATION

*It's the Lord's desire that the supernatural territory we occupy,
the realms of life where we consistently demonstrate His
authority, grow larger and more powerful as we pass it on to the
next generation. Inheritance is a biblical concept... It enables
the next generation to start where the previous generation left
off. — Bill Johnson, The Supernatural Power of a Transformed
Mind*[20]

I come from a background of spiritual poverty. Growing up in communist Russia I couldn't boast about having a legacy of previous generations who would testify about the faithfulness of God. I was the first one in my family to come to faith in Jesus. I experienced a different kind of spiritual parenting through a missionary couple, George and Donna Snow, who were in their 50's at that time. They came to live in Krasnoyarsk, Siberia, so they could explain the Bible to people who, like me, were previously taught that Jesus was a mythical figure and now were hungry to know the truth. I am so thankful that they came to be that relay leg in my race to bridge the spiritual gap that existed between generations in my own country. To this day, in their mid-seventies, they fly all over the world to minister and speak restoration into people's lives. They are internationally sought out counselors who minister truth, love and deliverance. My husband and I recently had the privilege to spend a few days with them. As I drove them back to the airport, I told them, "Whenever you decide to stop, you know it is not going to end. It is a relay race." My Dear Marathoner, I have grabbed a hold of their baton and I will not let go until my part of the race is done.

Meditation and prayer:

Think about people whose spiritual walk helped you build your own foundation in God. What kind of things have you learned from their lives and their examples? How can you expand on that with your own life in order to be a link for the next generation? Pray that God will give you wisdom and grace to fulfill this great responsibility.

Week 9: A RELAY RACE

Day 4 (Short Run, Speed Training 6 miles) THE MARK OF LEGACY

> *I want to leave a legacy. How will they remember me?*
> *Did I chose to love?*
> *Did I point to you enough to make a mark on things?*
> *I want to leave an offering...*
> *— Legacy, Song Lyrics[21]*

Whether you are aware of it or not you are leaving footprints behind you as you are running forward. What kind of legacy are you leaving and what would you like it to be? Do you want to go beyond the "temporary trappings of this world," as the song goes? Does the value of a person's life depend on how much education, possessions, money, experiences and prestige one acquires throughout life? Or is it defined by how much one gives to others?

During the "speed training" challenge today write out the things you think make your life valuable. What do you want to be remembered by? What can you begin doing right now to make sure your legacy is one worth leaving for those coming behind you?

Week 9: A RELAY RACE

Day 5 (Short Run 5 miles) SPIRITUAL FATHERHOOD

> — *Do you feel like it messed up your childhood not having a dad?*
> — *More than you know...*
> *Courageous. A dialog between David Tomson and Nathan Hayes*[22]

In Day 3 this week I told you about the missionary couple who filled the role of my spiritual parents. If they hadn't taken the time to mentor me and serve as a godly example, I wouldn't be where I am right now. As much as this generation is desperate for good natural fathers, the need for spiritual fathers is just as crucial. Don't wait until you feel like you have already run most of your race and have achieved God's purposes for your life to step into a role of a spiritual father or mother, although if you are there this entry is really for you. You don't need to be perfect either. If you have a passion for God and like to encourage others, then there are spiritually "fatherless" and "motherless" people out there who are searching for guidance and wisdom that you have to share. And if you are a person who senses the absence of spiritual leadership in your life, pray and ask God to send you a spiritual father or mother. Once you have someone on your heart, don't be afraid to approach them and ask them to mentor you.

Week 9: A RELAY RACE

Day 6 (Short Run 4 miles) THE BATON

I pray also that the eyes of your heart may be enlightened in order that you may know the hope to which he has called you, the riches of his glorious inheritance in the saints, and his incomparably great power for us who believe. — *Ephesians 1:18 (NIV)*

My Dear Marathoner, I'd like to reiterate the lesson of Week 1 to you: we run the race not because we have to but because we are summoned and drawn by a higher calling. Our baton is a baton of hope, glory and power. That's His rich inheritance that God desires for us to get a hold of and pass on to others during our race.

What kind of riches can you identify in your spiritual inheritance? How can you apply them and build on them, so that what once seemed to be an impossible reach for you becomes a norm to you and your natural and spiritual children? One of the blessings of my spiritual inheritance is that God can heal physical illnesses. As I pray for sick people in the name of Jesus and see results I increase my faith inheritance. Consequently, my children will be able to know God in the area of healing even more than I did. It can be other things as well: having a functional family, living free of substance abuse, finding God's love and being used by Him. Whatever your baton may be, run with it and pass it on to the next generation.

Week 9: A RELAY RACE

Day 7 (Short Run 4 miles, Meditation) THE ANCHOR

*I tell you the truth, anyone who has faith in me will do what I
have been doing. He will do even greater things than these,
because I am going to the Father. — John 14:12 (NIV)*

In a relay race the strongest and fastest runner (referred to
as the anchor) usually gets to run the last leg of the relay. This
racing strategy helps me better understand verses like "The
glory of this present house will be greater than the glory of the
former house," (Haggai 2:9) and "In the last days, God says, I
will pour out my Spirit on all people." (Acts 2:17a) God is
saving His best for last; He will ensure that His church finishes
with a bang. As believers in the new covenant we get to be a
part of all this: "Your sons and daughters will prophesy, your
young men will see visions, your old men will dream dreams."
(Acts 2:17b) We are called to be the anchor and we can be the
strongest and fastest racers by the power of His Holy Spirit.
Jesus really meant it when He said we'd do the same things and
even greater things than He did! I am not promoting some
teaching on the end of the world here. All I want to say is that
God wants you to run as if you are an anchor, and the purpose
of the Holy Spirit in your life is to help you become that anchor
by releasing God's power through your life. We can reveal His
glory to the world if we believe and accept His call and allow
Him to fill us with the Holy Spirit.

My Dear Marathoner, this is where my faith marathon
training challenge lies: in the deep-seated and profound
pursuit of getting everything God wants us to have. Does doing
the same and greater things than Jesus sound radical to you?
Do you feel inadequate? During your prayer and meditation
time talk to God about how you could become His faith anchor
in your generation.

Week 10: CHEERING FROM THE SIDELINES

Day 1 (Long Run 12 miles) THE CLOUD OF WITNESSES

Therefore, since we are surrounded by such a great cloud of witnesses, let us throw off everything that hinders and the sin that so easily entangles, and let us run with perseverance the race marked out for us. — Hebrews 12:1 (NIV)

You may have noticed I already used the verse quoted above earlier in the devotional. This time, I want to draw your attention to the "great cloud of witnesses." Someone else came to watch you race and cheer you on. The Message Bible calls them "the veterans" and "the pioneers."   In order to understand who came to yell "Go, _____ (fill in your name here)!" you need to read Hebrews chapter 11. It is those who where commended for their faith for being certain of what they did not see (Hebrews 11:1-2): Abel, Enoch, Noah, Abraham, Isaac, Jacob, Joseph, Moses, Joshua, Rahab, Gideon, Barak, Samson, Jephthah, David, Samuel, and the prophets.   I encourage you to study every one of them on your own time to discover how their faith was pleasing to God.

One of the reasons I enjoyed the Marine Corps Marathon was the unfading enthusiasm and support of spectators along every mile of the race. Their cheering uplifted, entertained and inspired. One of my favorite posters or banners along the way was "It's not your sweat, it's your fat cells crying."   The banner's humor distracted me from the strain I was feeling. I wonder, if Moses were to hold a banner during my spiritual race, what would it say?

My Dear Marathoner, how does it feel to know that your race is being watched? I sometimes feel like hiding when I think about the fact that I am observed not by mere spectators but by the experts who graduated with distinction and honors. And yet, I know they are watching in awe. They never got to

91

experience what we have in Christ. In fact, Hebrews 11:40 says that "only with us would they be made perfect." Their race is officially over only after all of us new covenant believers cross the finish line. It's no wonder why they are cheering. During this week use your imagination to think of the banner slogans some of them may be holding up for you.

Week 10: CHEERING ON THE SIDELINES

Day 2 (Short Run 4 miles) BANNER # 1: IF THE LORD IS GOD, FOLLOW HIM

Elijah went before the people and said, "How long will you waver between two opinions? If the Lord is God, follow him; but if Baal is God, follow him." — 1 Kings 18:21 (NIV)

The prophet Elijah knew something about supernatural running. You can read in 1 Kings 18:46 about how the power of God came upon him and he ran ahead of Ahab's chariot to Jezreel. I wish I could experience something like that during my next marathon! Elijah was a man who led a supernatural lifestyle with full dependence on God and in radical obedience to Him. He spoke boldly and presented his challenge with God's authority. You can read in 1 Kings 18 about how Elijah stood up to the wicked king Ahab and 450 prophets of Baal and how the Lord answered powerfully by consuming a bull sacrifice that had been drenched in water. Elijah's message to these people was to abandon their idols and worship the true God. "If the Lord is God, follow Him." Let this banner empower you on your run.

Week 10: CHEERING ON THE SIDELINES

Day 3 (Short Run 3 miles, Meditation) BANNER 2: BEHOLD THE ONE WHO IS INVISIBLE

By faith he (Moses) left Egypt, not fearing the king's anger; he persevered because he saw him who is invisible. — Hebrews 11:27 (NIV)

Moses accomplished great things for the nation of Israel because he was confident in the One with whom he spoke with to face to face. He was aware of his identity in God and his calling. He knew what it was like to boldly come into a place of intimacy with the Lord. In fact, when Moses begged God to send His Presence with the people of Israel, he received an incredible response: "I will do the very thing you have asked, because I am pleased with you and I know you by name." (Exodus 33:17) What did Moses ask for in return? "Now, show me your glory." (v 18). Amazingly, even though God said Moses couldn't see His face and live, he received an affirmative answer. As a result, God caused "all His goodness" to pass in front of Moses, and He proclaimed His name in front of him (read 33:19-34:10).

When you ask God to reveal Himself to You, He is willing to have all His goodness pass before you! You need to be able to see it with your eyes of faith in order to succeed in your journey. His name has been proclaimed to us as Jesus Christ, the Savior. He is merciful and compassionate, slow to anger and abounding in love (Exodus 34:6).

Meditation and prayer:

Focus your eyes of faith on God's goodness. Make a mental list of how good God has been to you. Proclaim His goodness in your prayer and worship.

Week 10: CHEERING ON THE SIDELINES

Day 4 (Short Run, Speed Training 5 miles) BANNER 3: GOD HAS PROVIDED THE SACRIFICE

Abraham believed God and it was credited to him as righteousness, and he was called God's friend. — James 2:23 (NIV)

Abraham demonstrated his faith by being willing to offer up his son Isaac on the altar as a sacrifice (Genesis 22). As a parent you might and should think *what a horrible and unjust thing to ask!* Yet, Abraham saw with the eyes of faith that God would "provide the lamb for the burnt offering" (v 8). He received the revelation that is so easily accessible to us through Christ. As he passed the test and God told him to let Isaac go, Abraham's heart must have identified with the heart of God who, later, willingly let His only begotten Son die on the cross for our sins. It was neither just nor fair for Jesus to die in our place, but He still did because of His love for us.

My Dear Marathoner, there is a reason why I chose to use Abraham's banner in the Speed Training section. 1 Thessalonians 5:10 says, "He died for us so that, whether we are awake or asleep, we may live together with him." God has already provided a sacrifice for us to live with Him every day of our lives. Are you going to step out and make your faith complete by acting on this truth like Abraham did and live your life with Him and for Him based on the perfect sacrifice He has already provided? Do you see the Invisible clearly enough that you are willing to give Him your all?

Week 10: CHEERING ON THE SIDELINES

Day 5 (Short Run 5 miles) BANNER 4: EMBRACE A NEW IDENTITY BY FAITH

Her (Rahab's) exercise of faith did not come after Rahab went to rehab. She was actively making a living as a prostitute when she decided that she might just believe God over her own press. You see, that's the beauty of the story! — Beth Moore, Believing God[23]

Hebrews 11:31 tells us about Rahab the following: "By faith the prostitute Rahab, because she welcomed the spies, was not killed with those who were disobedient." In the time of decision she acted upon what she'd heard about God's power, telling the spies, "I know that the Lord has given this land to you and that a great fear of you has fallen on us." (Joshua 2:9) As a result, she was saved and received a new identity that we can find in Matthew 1:5: Salmon, the father of Boaz, whose mother was Rahab. She became a part of the genealogy of the Savior! That's what God intended for her from the very beginning; she stepped into her destiny through her faith in the power of Almighty God. In the New Testament, her old identity as a prostitute is only mentioned as a part of her faith testimony.

My Dear Marathoner, when you accept Jesus by faith, He changes your identity. He doesn't call you by your old name "sinner" anymore. You are His child and His heir.

Week 10: CHEERING ON THE SIDELINES

Day 6 (Short Run 5 miles) BANNER 5: MAY HE GIVE YOU THE DESIRE OF YOUR HEART AND MAKE ALL YOUR PLANS SUCCEED!

I have found David son of Jesse a man after my own heart; he will do everything I want him to do. — Acts 13:22 (NIV)

King David messed up big time. Yet, he is remembered as a man of faith who pleased God. Just read the book of Psalms and you will discover why. The extravagant praise that David lavished on God boldly declares the revelation of who He really is. I encourage you to use some of David's expressions in the book of Psalms and let your own praise put God in His rightful place over your circumstances.

In the meantime, be encouraged by David's blessing that comes out of his personal experience of pursuing God: "May the Lord answer you when you are in distress; may the name of the God of Jacob protect you. May he send you help from the sanctuary and grant you support from Zion. May he remember all your sacrifices and accept your burnt offerings. May he give you the desire of your heart and make all your plans succeed. We will shout for joy when you are victorious and will lift up our banners in the name of our God. May the Lord grant all your requests." (Psalm 20:1-5)

Week 10: CHEERING ON THE SIDELINES

Day 7 (Rest Day, Meditation) BANNER 6: THE BANQUET HALL AWAITS

He has taken me to the banquet hall, and his banner over me is love. — Song of Songs 2:4 (NIV)

Behind the finish line after a marathon runners can always count on finding a smorgasbord of bagels, bananas and even a beer station! During the Marine Corps Marathon I saw banners that encouraged runners to keep going to the finish just to get to that nice cold can of beer. There is a wedding feast that awaits us at the end of our race (Revelation 19:9), but God has promised to provide refreshments along the way as well! Jesus is waving His own banner over us during the race. It spells "L-O-V-E." He wants us to partake of it, to feast on it as we run. His love is our refreshment station at any point during our race. In fact, the more we stop for it, the better shape we will be in at the end. And we do need to be in a good shape since we are being presented to Him as a Bride. At the end of my runs I am always the least presentable, drenched in sweat, red faced and stinky. Somehow though, in His eyes, the Bride that finishes the race is the one that is ready for Him, mature, and thoroughly pleasing. (Song of Songs, 8:10)

My Dear Marathoner, during your rest day today ask Jesus to reveal to you the banquet feast He has prepared for you. Remember that it is not just for the end of the race: He wants you to get a taste of it any time you want throughout your race. Partake of the richness of His love every day – even in the times of adversity, so you can say as King David, "You prepare a table before me in the presence of my enemies" (Psalm 23:5a).

Week 11: YOUR FIRST 20-MILER

Day 1 (Long Run 20 miles) PERSEVERANCE DEFINED

Perseverance is the hard work you do after you get tired of doing the hard work you already did. — Newt Gingrich[24]

Never tire of doing what is right. — 2 Thessalonians 3:13 (NIV)

I did my first 10 miles without noticing. Consistent training was paying off. I would not say I needed to exercise perseverance in the first half of the run. Then my legs started gradually feeling tight, my clothes were drenched in sweat, and my mind became helplessly bored. Somewhere between miles 16 and 18 I started frequently asking myself, "when is this going to be over?"

When you are just starting something, whether you enjoy it or not, it may not seem very hard. But eventually the adrenaline wears off, the reality of your circumstances sets in, difficulties arise and your mind begins to question if it is all worthwhile. That's when, if you choose to stay the right course, you are starting to persevere.

Hebrews 10:35-36 says: "So do not throw away your confidence; it will be richly rewarded. You need to persevere so that when you have done the will of God, you will receive what he has promised." It is very easy to lose confidence in the significance of what you are doing and in your ability to reach the goal when you are exhausted. The devil wants to use tests and trials to steal our joy and confidence. God's purpose for allowing them is to make us mature and strong. When I am trying to endure the last few miles of my 20-mile run, it is very tempting to start thinking that I won't make it. Quitting all of a sudden looks like a viable option. The training that I've engaged in up to this point helps me stick with it. In the same way, if you have practiced the things I previously mentioned in this faith training devotional, you are prepared to handle your first 20-miler in a spiritual sense.

During your day or on your long run, think about what areas of your life you may have thrown away your confidence in God. Ask God to restore and strengthen your faith in those areas.

Week 11: YOUR FIRST 20-MILER

Day 2 (Rest Day, Meditation) A CALL REALLY TESTED

Consider it pure joy, my brothers, whenever you face trials of many kinds, because you know that the testing of your faith develops perseverance. Perseverance must finish its work so that you may be mature and complete, not lacking in anything. —
James 1:2-5

I have been running to overcome all my life. — Meb Keflezighi, Run to Overcome[25]

Do you feel like you've been pushing through a long race, constantly jumping over hurdles and overcoming adversity? Congratulations! According to the above verse, you have been going through the testing of your faith which is designed by God to bring you to a state of completion. I wish trials were not necessary but somehow it's only through overcoming the odds that we reach the full potential God has placed within us. If we persevere and maintain our faith in God's goodness and power in the middle of our difficulties we will not lack anything.

Meditation and prayer:

Think about the times in your life when you faced trials. How did they test your faith? Are you able to see the fruit of your perseverance with new levels of maturity and confidence in Him? God, I know You are here with me to help me overcome.

Week 11: YOUR FIRST 20-MILER

Day 3 (Short Run 5 miles) BLESSINGS OF PERSEVERANCE

Blessed is the man who perseveres under trial, because when he has stood the test, he will receive the crown of life that God has promised to those who love Him. — James 1:12 (NIV)

My Dear Marathoner, ask yourself what is going to happen if you persevere in the current matter that is so important to you. What will the results look like? The verse above comes right after James talks about the futility of earthly riches. God's best blessings do not come in material form. Perseverance in challenging times brings about the rewards that do not fade away like mere temporary things. These rewards have to do with our character, our faith and the quality of our relationships with God and others. If we persevere in our love for Him we get to be crowned with the crown of life. What an honor!

Week 11: YOUR FIRST 20-MILER

Day 4 (Short Run, Speed Training 6 miles) HERE COMES NOTHING

Perseverance is not a long race; it is many short races one after another. — Walter Elliott[26]

One of the mind tricks I play on myself when I am exhausted but need to keep pushing is telling myself, *here comes nothing!* I don't say, *look, you've already run 17 miles,* because I don't want to focus on the reason for my exhaustion. Instead, I assure myself, *you only have 3 miles to go, here comes nothing.* I've done three mile runs many times before, and I know that for me they really do seem like nothing. So I keep repeating in my head at the end of a long run, *here comes nothing, now you only have two miles left instead of three,* and so on until I'm done.

I found that when you have persevered for a long time, it's easier to just look at the goal that's right ahead of you and break it down into small steps. If you've run any long distance you understand that those last few miles seem to drag the longest and you get more and more tired after each one of them. If the finish seems far away because your strength is spent, encourage yourself by saying "Here comes nothing!" Remember, you made it to this point by the grace of God to begin with. It is the grace of God that will take you to the end.

During your "speed workout" think of a challenge you might be facing right now and break it down into smaller tasks or steps. Then say to yourself "Here comes nothing!" regarding any circumstances that seem especially daunting to you. You will overcome them one "short race" at a time.

Week 11: YOUR FIRST 20-MILER

Day 5 (Short Run 3 miles) STICK WITH IT

We can do anything we want to do if we stick to it long enough.
— *Hellen Keller*[27]

Don't discard a goal or stop trying just because the only thing you've seen so far is failure. If you know God is calling you to something, stick with it despite the challenges. The result of such perseverance is like the gigantic bucket at a water park that my kids like to play under. The water is dripping into the bucket little by little but the bucket doesn't turn upside down until it is full. It seems like nothing is happening, but then all of a sudden the bucket tips and the water crashes down on the giggling and screaming children and adults that have been waiting underneath. If you are standing at the right place, you will not escape the big splash. God will not withhold His power from those who refuse to quit.

Week 11: YOUR FIRST 20-MILER

Day 6 (Short Run 6 miles) COVER THE DISTANCE

*I will give you every place where you set your foot. — Joshua
1:3a (NIV)*

Circumstances may not change but we will. Even if we don't see outward results right away, there are things that happen in the spiritual realm through our perseverance. Just like a runner covers distance while running, we possess spiritual territory by being steadfast. We take ownership in places where our feet go in a spiritual sense: we pray for things to take place and for issues to be resolved and as we persevere in faith, we see God opening doors of opportunity for us to have an impact in those areas. Communities, work places and individuals we've been praying for become a part of our sphere of influence when we demonstrate and share His love, power, and presence.

Week 11: YOUR FIRST 20-MILER

Day 7 (Rest Day, Meditation) CHANGED THROUGH PERSEVERANCE

You may have had to suffer grief in all kinds of trials. These have come so that your faith – of greater worth than gold, which perishes even though refined by fire – may be proved genuine and may result in praise, glory and honor when Jesus Christ is revealed. — 1 Peter 1:6b-7 (NIV)

I am just amazed at my body. It ran for over 3 hours the other day on my 20 mile run. Thinking back, I am in awe at what it had to endure. Of course, I trained it through consistent long distance running which helped increase my muscular and cardiovascular endurance. Every long distance run prior to that was like a refining process but that 20-miler was truly a refiner's fire. Even though I usually run for enjoyment, I couldn't call the last 4 or 5 miles of that run entertaining! In the same way, in order to mature, our faith needs to go through the refining furnace that is not always fun, and it needs to do it more than one time. When gold is refined it must be put through fire in order to melt away all the impurities. It continues to go through fire over and over again until the Master Refiner can look into it and see His reflection. If we want our faith to have substance, we need to submit to the refining process and let God take us on those "20-miler" faith adventures where our spiritual life is tested.

My Dear Marathoner, what does your 20-mile test run look like right now? In other words, what areas in your life require perseverance at the moment? During your meditation today pray and ask God to give you understanding of how He wants to refine you in your faith journey. Don't be afraid to submit to His challenge; when you look back after a while you will be amazed at His work of transformation in you.

Week 12: DOES POSITIVE THINKING REALLY WORK?

Day 1 (Long Run 13 miles) ACCORDING TO HIS POWER WITHIN US

Now to him who is able to do immeasurably more than all we ask or imagine, according to his power that is at work within us, to him be glory in the church and in Christ Jesus throughout all generations, for ever and ever! — Ephesians 3:20-21 (NIV)

My friend who had a baby a few months before I gave birth to my first child encouraged me before the delivery: "The main thing is to think positively and everything will go smoothly." Well, after several hours of back labor, violent vomiting and a stalled dilating process, my positive thinking didn't get me very far. An emergency C-section put me out of my misery. When you are dealing with intense pain and your body's functions or other circumstances are out of your control, it's not always possible to think positively. And even if you manage to do so, it may not change things a bit.

Running is much easier than labor, even if it's a marathon. But even in long distance running positive thinking is useless in some instances. No matter how much you psych yourself up, you can't do anything if your body decides to bonk. I have a friend who once went on a run and felt so great he wanted to do 10 miles without any prior preparation or access to drinking fluids along his route. Despite how good he felt in the beginning, all of a sudden his legs gave out and he found himself crawling on the side of the road in desperate need of water. Another friend of mine fainted a mile before the end of her first half marathon. As paramedics were carrying her away to the ambulance she was half-consciously telling them to let her go so that she could finish the race. I can admire her will power and determination, but unfortunately they were not enough to get her to her goal.

My Dear Marathoner, I'm sorry if I sound like I am trying to rain on your parade. If this whole devotional is to encourage and not to discourage you, why am I making this point? There are so many motivational self-help books out there that are trying to convince you that if you think positively everything will come together nicely for you. I hope you are catching on by now that even though I have been challenging you all along to train yourself to think correctly, glorified positive thinking is not what gets the job done. It is the power of God within you. Our thinking and imagination are limited; He is not. We need to consistently rely on His guidance and wisdom. By the way, both of my friends mentioned above have successfully completed other long distance races since then.

During your meditation today or on your long run be honest with yourself and think of examples in your own life when positive thinking was not enough. I would recommend that you memorize Ephesians 3:20-21 and meditate frequently on the fact that you've been empowered by Him to fulfill His plan for your life.

Week 12: DOES POSITIVE THINKING REALLY WORK?

Day 2 (Short Run 6 miles) STINKING THINKING?

Denial is the fruit of fear, not the root of faith. True faith can evaluate the circumstances without growing hopeless because it sees the world through God's eyes. — Kris Vallotton, Spirit Wars[28]

Well, positive thinking doesn't always get us far, but negative thinking, or, what I call "stinking thinking," almost certainly causes us to fall several steps behind. Please, don't get all pessimistic on me here just because the formula doesn't always get you the right answer. I've noticed that each time I dwell on a stressful situation during my run, it sucks the energy right out of me, my breathing becomes laborious, my legs get heavier and I feel like quitting. Conversely, when I meditate on God's word and talk with Him in my thoughts regarding the same situation, I don't even notice how I get from one point on my route to another. In order to grow in faith, you need the kind of thinking that honestly assesses your situation but then looks for God's opinion and solutions with hope.

Week 12: DOES POSITIVE THINKING REALLY WORK?

Day 3 (Rest Day, Meditation) THE MIND OF CHRIST

For who has known the mind of the Lord that he may instruct him? But we have the mind of Christ. — 1 Corinthians 2:16 (NIV)

Earlier in 1 Corinthians 2 Paul says that "no one knows the thoughts of God except the Spirit of God" (v. 11), and the Spirit of God lives in God's children. We can accept and understand God's wisdom through His Spirit inside of us. It is the kind of thinking that an outsider may consider nonsense or foolishness but it makes complete sense to us and gives us the necessary wisdom for our needs and circumstances. Some examples of this can be forgiving someone when the natural tendency would be to retaliate, abstaining from sex before marriage, putting money in the offering during tight financial times and staying calm when things fall apart. If we follow biblical principles and stay in tune with the Holy Spirit, God' wisdom will guide us into right decisions and outcomes we will not regret later.

Meditation and prayer:

Father, please help me to recognize the mind of Christ within me and to always seek Your wisdom.

Week 12: DOES POSITIVE THINKING REALLY WORK?

Day 4 (Short Run, Speed Training 6 miles) WHAT ABOUT POSITIVE TALKING?

The good man brings good things out of the good stored up in his heart, and the evil man brings evil things out of the evil stored up in his heart. For out of the overflow of his heart his mouth speaks. — Luke 6:45 (NIV)

What makes one person, as soon as problems arise, pick up a phone and lament for hours to a friend or complain about them all day at the office? And what makes another one speak hope and trust in God in the midst of difficult circumstances? The latter, instead of picking up the phone, first got down on his knees and talked to God.

My Dear Marathoner, today my challenge for you is to pour out your heart to God about your problem. You can be free to tell Him how unbearable it is. Once you are done, store up the "good" in your heart by mentally listing or journaling all the great things He has done and will do for you until your understanding overflows with the revelation of who He is and His power to bring you through your difficulties into victory. Then your mouth will speak a totally different message. The declaration of your tongue uttered in faith will come to pass, as Jesus said, "Have faith in God... if anyone says to this mountain, 'Go, throw yourself into the sea,' and doesn't doubt in his heart but believes that what he says will happen, it will be done for him." (Mark 11:22-23).

Week 12: DOES POSITIVE THINKING REALLY WORK?

Day 5 (Short Run 5 miles) THINK BY FAITH

No eye has seen, no ear has heard, no mind has conceived what God has prepared for those who love him – but God has revealed it to us by his Spirit. — 1 Corinthians 2:9-10 (NIV)

Don't just try to think positive thoughts. Strengthen your faith by listening to and becoming sure of what God's Spirit within you is telling you about what He has prepared for you. Write out Bible verses that directly relate to your situation and meditate on them. Over time you will develop a deep sense of confidence that in any situation you can step out and obey His guidance and He will never let you down. To think positively by faith means to live in a state of unwavering expectation that God will always move on your behalf.

Week 12: DOES POSITIVE THINKING REALLY WORK?

Day 6 (Short Run 5 miles) QUESTIONING HEAVEN

Awake, O Lord! Why do you sleep? Rouse yourself! Do not reject us forever. Why do you hide your face and forget our misery and oppression? — Psalm 44:23-24 (NIV)

Go ahead and vent to God. He knows all your thoughts anyway; He knows exactly how you feel. Nothing you tell Him is going to shock Him. Why be religious and hide how you feel? I believe God would rather you talk openly to Him and build your relationship with Him than shove your questions and doubts under a rug and slowly lose your trust in His goodness.

Week 12: DOES POSITIVE THINKING REALLY WORK?

Day 7 (Short Run 4 miles, Meditation) GODLY WISDOM THAT WORKS

Who is wise and understanding among you? Let him show it by his good life, by deeds done in humility that comes from wisdom. — James 3:13 (NIV)

No matter how positively you think, you still need to live your faith out. You need to act on what you believe is true. Positive thinking that really works is always rooted in godly wisdom. Perseverance, faith and wisdom are interconnected and all three are signs of maturity. You act in wisdom and faith when you choose to persevere and as a result you gain even more wisdom and your faith matures. Perseverance is impossible without faith. Faith is like the wind that blows in our sails and keeps us going.

During your meditation time today think about the things you believe about who God is and who you are through Him. Do you feel God prompting you to act upon any of those beliefs, especially in areas you've never stepped out in before? For example, if you believe that God is a healer and Jesus commanded His disciples to pray for the sick, would you go and pray for someone who needs healing? If you believe that God is forgiving and He wants us to make peace with others, would you go to someone you've wronged and ask for their forgiveness? Make positive thinking work for you by actively obeying the truth.

Week 13: GO FOR THE GOLD

Day 1 (Long Run 20 miles) DON'T SETTLE FOR THE MEDIOCRE

You give me your shield of victory, and your right hand sustains me; you stoop down to make me great. — Psalm 18:35 (NIV)

This week's title could have been the title of this entire devotional. Just go for the gold! At the time of writing this, there is a growing anticipation around the world for the start of the 2012 Olympic Games in London. Millions of people will gather around their television sets to watch and cheer on the best athletes in the world. Why are the Olympic Games so compelling to watch? I believe it's not just because they display such amazing athletic talent. It is because of the athletes' passionate quest for the gold; to be the best they can be. A wide range of every possible human emotion that this quest evokes in its competitors deeply resonates with the spectators as well. All of us who are watching could relate on some level to the joy and pride of the Olympians' victories and to the agony of their defeats. Whether we are aware of it or not, deep down in our souls we long to go after God's gold and fulfill His purposes for our lives. The cry of my heart is that those who read this book will be challenged deep in their core to go beyond their comfort zone and strive for God's best for their lives, even for what they thought was impossible.

I tend to go by the principle that says, "Why run a half-marathon when you can do the whole thing?" It shows a part of me that always wants to have it all. But I understand that not everyone can commit to marathon training due to time constraints, physical challenges and other factors. A half-marathon and even a 5K are quite viable and honorable options. You can certainly run a 5K and still go for your best. It's the same thing in life. Everyone sets different sized goals and it is important we give even small matters our greatest effort. On the other hand, don't be intimidated if you know He wants you to set your bar higher. In fact, in most cases, God sets the bar much higher than we do for ourselves. He sees our potential and what He wants to accomplish through us by His power much better than we do. Refuse to settle for just "good" when "perfect" is given to you through Christ. No Olympic athlete, when given a choice, would pick a bronze over gold. Refuse to settle for simply "good" when Christ offers to make you great. Let's go for the gold together!

My Dear Marathoner, instead of prayer and meditation during this long run, please tell me and others your story on Facebook or Twitter. You've made it to this point in your faith training and I would love to hear about how you are doing in your quest for God's gold. I am honored to know that you are my training partner.

Week 13: GO FOR THE GOLD

Day 2 (Short Run 3 miles) PERFECTIONISM

Don't be deceived, my dear brothers. Every good and perfect gift is from above, coming down from the Father of the heavenly lights, who does not change like shifting shadows. — James 1:16-17 (NIV)

My Dear Marathoner, please do not confuse excellence with perfectionism. Have you ever gotten an A- in class and were frustrated with yourself that you didn't earn an A? For those of us who are used to doing things well and excelling at them it is not easy to accept the fact that we don't always get to accomplish things at a hundred percent success rate. Our own mistakes and the errors of others are frustrating and can eat at us for days or even years. Yet, on the road to His excellence and holiness, Jesus wants to set us free from perfectionism. He teaches us that He is the key to our success, whether it is in business, marriage, school or ministry. When we acknowledge our own imperfections and trust Him with our personal growth, we gain an ability to give grace to ourselves and others. Perfectionism will ruin you but the pursuit of His excellence will give you life.

Week 13: GO FOR THE GOLD

Day 3 (Rest Day, Meditation) BETTER IS ONE DAY IN YOUR COURTS

Better is one day in your courts than a thousand elsewhere; I would rather be a doorkeeper in the house of my God than dwell in the tents of the wicked. — Psalm 84:10 (NIV)

I love chocolate. In my opinion, some of the more expensive kinds taste the best, especially European bars. I must guiltily admit that dark chocolate lies behind some of my writing inspirations. After each appointment at my dentist's I usually get a "goody bag" that contains a sample of floss and toothpaste and a sugar-free chocolate tooth. I tell you, the tooth is not only sugar free; it's taste free as well! It doesn't even melt in your mouth! If you have recently had some excellent chocolate you would despise the taste of that fake chocolate imitation. (I hope my dentist doesn't read this!)

Leading a sinful lifestyle apart from God is like eating that fake chocolate tooth. Scripture invites us to "taste and see that the Lord is good." (Ps 34:8a) The rest of Psalm 84 declares that God withholds no good thing "from those whose walk is blameless." His "good" is so much better than our own good. If we try to make our life work apart from His influence we can only get so far. But if we choose His way and abide in His courts we get a genuine experience of the real deal, not the fake imitation. Notice that the "courts" refer to the temple where David appointed four thousand gatekeepers to praise God with musical instruments and singing (1 Chronicles 15:16 and 23:5). When we praise God we cast down our own crowns and acknowledge that all our talents, accomplishments and all the good things we have ultimately belong to Him (Revelation 4:9-11). I believe that when He receives our crowns, He makes them even greater and more glorious, so "those who seek the Lord lack no good thing." (Ps 34:10b)

Meditation and prayer:

Join the heavenly praise found in Revelation 4:10-11: "You are worthy, our Lord and God, to receive glory and honor and power, for you created all things, and by your will they were created and have their being." God, I give you all of me and I want all of You. Being in your presence is better than anything else.

Week 13: GO FOR THE GOLD

Day 4 (Short Run, Speed Training 6 miles) DON'T DISREGARD YOUR FIRST MILE

Who despises the day of small things? — Zechariah 4:10 (NIV)

Sometimes it seems like we run hard but we haven't gone far. Don't get frustrated with yourself if running one mile is the farthest you can go right now. Stick with it and you'll be able to do more. It's easy to give up when we don't see great results immediately but even small changes can gradually grow into something significant. We have a promise that "hope does not disappoint us, because God has poured out his love into our hearts by the Holy Spirit, whom he has given us." (Romans 5:5)

My Dear Marathoner, what areas in your life do you seem to be unable to progress past the first mile? How can you make sure you are doing your best during that "first mile" and that you don't give up, so that eventually you break through farther?

Week 13: GO FOR THE GOLD

Day 5 (Short Run 5 miles) LUCKY OR BLESSED?

Praise be to the God and Father of our Lord Jesus Christ, who has blessed us in the heavenly realms with every spiritual blessing in Christ. — Ephesians 1:3 (NIV)

How does one move from the realm of good to the realm of great? Some people would say that a certain amount of luck is necessary. I disagree. Luck is accidental, but blessing is intentional. Luck is temporal: it can be found but it can also easily be lost. Blessings are constant and unfailing because they are coming from a reliable source. We just need to realize that the word "blessing" means more than wishing someone well when they sneeze. How powerful is God's blessing really? In his attempt to get a hold of the blessing Jacob was willing to commit a low act of deception toward his own father and brother (Genesis 27). Did he know something we don't? He was aware that his father's blessing determined his destiny. Later in life, Jacob was prophetically particular about the way he blessed Joseph's sons (Genesis 48), and his blessing came to pass. I am glad we don't have to lie and trick anyone to receive our blessings. God gave them all to us through Christ. I can do all things through Christ because I am blessed by Him. He predestined you and me for greatness.

Week 13: GO FOR THE GOLD

Day 6 (Short Run 6 miles) MORE PRECIOUS THAN GOLD

The fear of the Lord is clean, enduring forever; the judgments of the Lord are true; they are righteous altogether. They are more desirable than gold, yes than much fine gold... — Psalm 19:9-10a (NASB)

God's judgments are more desirable than gold? Am I missing something? Aren't we supposed to fear judgment? We are all going to be judged whether we want to be or not. The good news for us who are followers of Christ is that through Jesus the court's decision is going to be in our favor. We are forever declared righteous and have become undeservedly sentenced to His mercy, grace, and blessings because of the blood of Christ. The litigations, if you will, are not fair. They are biased toward us because of the cross. Jesus took our place of punishment and shame for us. These kinds of judgments are better than winning gold at the end of the race. Choose to proudly wear His favor around your neck like a medal.

Week 13: GO FOR THE GOLD

Day 7 (Rest Day, Meditation) I WILL COME FORTH AS GOLD

But he knows the way that I take; when he has tested me, I will come forth as gold. — Job 23:10 (NIV)

When we go through the testing of our faith we want to come out as gold: pure, strong, and of great value. Gold attracts because it shines. It doesn't corrode like other cheaper metals; it lasts. When our character is like gold the rains of life can come down on us and yet our lives show no signs of rust. We need to believe in the goodness and power of God in order to withstand every kind of pressure and shine in the end.

Meditation and Prayer:

Think of the times you've gone through the testing of your faith. How did that testing impact your life and your character to become more like gold? Father, make my faith to be like gold that coats me on the outside and fills me on the inside to protect me from the corruption of this world.

Week 14: IDENTITY CHECK

Day 1 (Long Run 13 miles) IN HIM

*He is not far from each one of us. For in him we live and move
and have our being. — Acts 17:27b-28a (NIV)*

Who or what do you identify yourself with? This morning as I drove to work in the morning I had to put on my behavioral-consultant-and-therapist hat. A few hours later I hurried home and put on my mommy hat while fixing snacks for my kids and arranging play dates. My husband came home and I got to wear my wife hat for a while until I flew out the door again to catch my long run with my marathoner hat on. Now it's late at night and I sit in front of my computer wearing an author hat and try to write this book. I wore all these hats in just one day, sometimes even attempting the exhausting feat of wearing more than one of them at the same time. Sound familiar? In the chaos of fulfilling my multiple important roles how do we define who we really are? Here is a small list of things the Bible says we are in Christ, no matter what hat we are wearing:

*For he chose us **in him** before the creation of the world to be holy and blameless in his sight. (Ephesians 1:4a)*

***In him** we have redemption through his blood, the forgiveness of sins... (Ephesians 1:7a)*

***In him** we were also chosen, having been predestined according to the plan of him who works out everything in conformity with the purpose of his will... (Ephesians 1:11)*

*Having believed, you were marked **in him** with a seal, the promised Holy Spirit. (Ephesians 1:13b)*

*Therefore, if anyone is **in Christ**, he is a new creation; the old has gone, the new has come! (2 Corinthians 5:17)*

*God made him who had no sin to be sin for us, so that **in him** we might become the righteousness of God. (2 Corinthians 5:21)*

*And **in Him** you were made complete, and He is the head over all rule and authority; (Colossians 2:10, NASB)*

My Dear Marathoner, this list of verses could go on and on. No matter what hat you wear throughout the day, identify yourself with Christ. During your long run today or throughout the day meditate on one of these verses and what it means to you to be in Him.

Week 14: IDENTITY CHECK

Day 2 (Short Run 6 miles) SUPERNATURAL RUNNERS

Simba, you have forgotten me. You have forgotten who you are and so forgotten me. — Mufasa, The Lion King[29]

Even if you are training for your first marathon, by this time in your training I hope you are beginning to see yourself as a marathoner. Others are starting to see you that way too. It's no wonder: just think about how many miles you ran last weekend! It's hard for me to see myself as a marathon runner even though I am training for my third one. Maybe it's my old self-image that inhibits me from seeing myself in that way. Probably, somewhere in the back of my mind I am still a girl that hated running and couldn't run a mile without getting out of breath. That's why sometimes in the back of my head I still say, "this just cannot be me." Yet, just like Mufasa in *The Lion King*, God doesn't want His children to live according to the false identity that we are unworthy, powerless and have no reason to care about fulfilling our life's true purpose. He wants us to realize that we are sons and daughters of a Mighty King who have free access to His glorious inheritance.

My Dear Marathoner, have you started seeing yourself as a *faith* marathoner and champion since you joined me on this faith training journey? You should by now. You are becoming a supernatural runner because through this training you are learning to rely on a higher reality and identify yourself with Christ. Don't let memories of past failures and mistakes talk you out of your new identity.

Week 14: IDENTITY CHECK

Day 3 (Rest Day, Meditation) CHILDREN OF GOD

How great is the love the Father has lavished on us, that we should be called children of God! And that is what we are! — 1 John 3:1 (NIV)

My daughter eagerly asked me to sign her up for the Kid's Marathon that will take place the day before my race in downtown Pittsburgh. It is a mile long run and she has never done anything like that before. At the age of seven she just wants to be like her mom. Alina has no real concept of how far one mile is but she doesn't question her ability to run it. Her running form is not perfect but in spite of that she is excited to do it and I am proud of her just for wanting to participate in the event regardless of how she does. My husband, her little brother and I will be there to loudly cheer her on!

God wants us to be in the race just so we can imitate Him. He doesn't want us to question our ability and He doesn't need us to be perfect. He wants us to trust like children do. Alina can enter the kid's race because I am participating in the adult marathon; she is participating in her race because she is my daughter. Let's imitate our Heavenly Father and run the race He prepared for us!

My Dear Marathoner, during your rest day meditate on the truth found in Mark 18:3: "Truly I say to you, unless you are converted and become like children, you will not enter the kingdom of heaven." (NASB). When you repent or become "converted," you become His child. In a healthy household children display a great deal of trust and a desire to imitate their parents. How much more should we trust and long to imitate our perfect Father!

Mediation and prayer:

I want to run the race with you, Daddy!

Week 14: IDENTITY CHECK

Day 4 (Short Run 4 miles, Speed Training) MORE THAN CONQUERORS

We are more than conquerors through him who loved us. —
Romans 8:37 (NIV)

My Dear Marathoner, the speed training challenge for you today is to learn how to roar like a lion. No, I haven't done it on any of my runs! I can only imagine people crossing to the other side of the street and giving me weird looks. When I think of a lion roaring, the Disney film *The Lion King* comes instantly to mind again. Little Simba is cornered by the mocking hyenas. He decides to stand up for himself and tries to roar. To his utter surprise, the perpetrators back up and flee. When the cub turns around he discovers that his father, Mufasa, is right behind him; it was his father's presence that scared the hyenas. Just like the little lion, we sometimes need to give a roar at the lies and negativity that the enemy is trying to discourage us with.

Even though I've never done any roaring while running I have done plenty of "roaring" in prayer. Jesus commissioned His disciples to walk in His power and promised to back them up with His authority (Matthew 28:18). He said that whatever they bound on earth would be bound in heaven and whatever they loosed on earth would be loosed in heaven (Matthew 16:19). When you are praying you can command your mountains to move, sickness to be healed, the lies of the enemy to be silenced and oppression to be lifted. You can declare your territory as a son or daughter of God. It's not arrogant! It's living by faith and knowing that there is a great lion right behind you backing you up.

Week 14: IDENTITY CHECK

Day 5 (Short Run 4 miles) SAINTS

For it is by grace you have been saved, through faith — and this is not from yourselves, it is the gift of God — not by works, so that no one can boast. — Ephesians 2:8-9 (NIV)

I have struggled with learning to see myself as a saint for a long time. Probably because such a title seemed far-fetched and belonged only to melancholy looking people painted on the walls of Orthodox and Catholic churches. If we are saved through the blood of Christ by faith, then exactly how holy are we? Can anything else but Jesus make us more holy? In 2 Corinthians 5:21 Paul writes: "God made him who had no sin to be sin for us, so that in him we might become the righteousness of God." In order to grow in our faith we need to embrace and accept the fact that Christ really did this for us and God truly sees us as saints through the blood of Christ: "The Father... has qualified you to share in the inheritance of the saints in the kingdom of light." (Colossians 1:12, NIV)

Week 14: IDENTITY CHECK

Day 6 *(Short Run 4 miles) GOD'S WORKMANSHIP*

For we are God's workmanship, created in Christ Jesus to do good works, which God prepared in advance for us to do. —
Ephesians 2:10 (NIV)

The word "workmanship" is the Hebrew word *melakah* and it means "work, business, workmen."[30] As I am writing this devotional it is becoming my piece of work and creation. I feel partial and protective about it. I want it to accomplish the purpose for which I am creating it: to encourage others in their pursuit of God. It will bring me great pleasure to know that it is serving its purpose and having an impact on others. In the same way, we are God's masterpiece. He is proud, partial and protective about us. We are His body, His hands and feet that will extend His Kingdom on this earth by fulfilling the call He has placed on our lives.

Week 14: IDENTITY CHECK

Day 7 (Short Run 4 miles, Meditation) THE MISSING LINK

If the Lord is with us, why has all this happened to us? Where are all his wonders that our fathers told us about...? — Judges 6:13 (NIV)

Yet there remains a distance between what should be and what will be. That distance is us! What will we be? We are the bridge between history and His story. — Kris Vallotton, The Supernatural Ways of Royalty[31]

My Dear Marathoner, we are destined to be the missing link between God's powerful truth and its realization on earth. Many people reject faith in God because they think God doesn't answer prayer. God desires for His word to become alive and active in you so that His power can operate freely in your life. His presence and reality become obvious and undeniable when we take Him at His word. God responded to Gideon by saying, "Go in the strength you have and save Israel out of Midian's hand. Am I not sending you?" (Judges 6:14) Let God's commission instill you with a sense of boldness that you can be the missing link wherever God sends you.

During your meditation today, think about what areas in your life still have a gap between what God's will is and what you see with your natural eyes. I am sure those areas are not hard to pinpoint. In addition, what other issues around you (in your culture, community, work, family, etc) stand out to you as being incongruent with Heaven's reality? Will you take a stand and pursue His manifested presence in those areas in your own life and the lives of others? If yes, write out a few of them that God is stirring up within you. Lift them up in prayer and ask God to give you guidance on how to become that missing link.

Week 15: THE MILEAGE PEAK

Day 1 (Long Run 20 miles) THE LAST 20-MILER AND THE CALL TESTED AGAIN

My sport is your sport's punishment. — Unknown (from a running poster)

To be honest, I am dreading my long run. I pace around the kitchen taking in small sips of water thinking about how daunting my task is this morning. Finally, I say to myself: "This is your last big push until the real deal," and head out the door. Two hours later my clothes are saturated and my arms are covered in dried up grits of sweat, my thighs are tight and my lips are dry. I still have about an hour more to go. I get off the running trail and dig through thick bush branches to find the sports drink I hid there earlier. I drink as I run without stopping. "It is crazy what I am doing to my body," I think, " and it's crazy what my body can do." Even though the end of the run seems like punishment it feels good to know that I did it. I made it through the three toughest runs in the training. I am ready for the big race.

The marathon training mileage usually peaks between weeks 11 and 15. For beginner and casual marathoners the toughest challenge involves at least three 20-mile runs. After the last long run during week 15 the mileage gradually starts to decrease. But what do mileage peaks look like in a faith training? I believe they come in the form of increased pressure on one's faith that could be either external or internal. Just like a marathoner needs more than one 20-mile run during training, we undergo multiple tests of our faith that make us stronger. Only we don't schedule them like in marathon training; life just throws them at us. What do we do when they arrive?

My Dear Marathoner, what seems like punishment to others has become your sport. You know what a "mileage peak" in your life means. You take it as an opportunity to grow. What is hard or impossible for most people is natural to you: believing God through it all regarding who He is, who you are, and what He can do through you. I am sure your circumstances, just like mine, are not perfect. They don't need to line up ideally at this point; you have enough momentum and motivation gathered up to soar through the toughest spots. You've built a solid foundation of trusting God and discipline that will keep your "spiritual legs" running. They will take you further than you've ever been. Keep your eyes on the goal and you will pass your faith tests in full victory.

On your long run or throughout your day meditate on this verse: "For whatever is born of God overcomes the world; and this is the victory that has overcome the world—our faith." (1 John 5:4, NASB)[32]

Week 15: THE MILEAGE PEAK

Day 2 (Rest Day, Meditation) WATCHING OUT FOR INJURIES

Above all else, guard your heart, for it is the wellspring of life. —
Proverbs 4:23 (NIV)

At this point in my training, I am trying to be very careful about my health. I am taking all of my vitamins and doing all my stretches. Last year I got knocked out right before the race by the flu. It weakened me so much I couldn't even walk a few steps without getting lightheaded. Fortunately, it was just a half-marathon, so I didn't put in as much effort to prepare as I have this year. The most frustrating and painful injuries and setbacks are the ones that happen to athletes before an important event and prevent them from achieving what they had been working so hard for.

My Dear Marathoner, please guard your heart from "injuries" during your training. The enemy will try to come in different ways to discourage you. His whole purpose is to make you feel disempowered and to keep you away from your destiny. As you've done in the early stages of training, keep yourself focused on God's truth and what He says about you. Be careful what you say and what you meditate on. Do not question His goodness to you and become double minded by swaying "to the right or the left." (Proverbs 4:24-27)

Meditation and prayer:

Ask the Holy Spirit to help you discern the ways the enemy is trying to discourage you in this stage of the game. What are his strategies and how can you specifically protect yourself from being injured?

Week 15: THE MILEAGE PEAK

Day 3 (Short Run 4 miles) BEYOND YOUR COMFORT ZONE

Pain is weakness leaving the body. — Unknown (from a running poster)

My Dear Marathoner, I am sure at this point you realize that comfort is not the word that best describes long distance running. I am amazed how in our western culture in this day and age we tend to think that whatever takes us out of our comfort zone is too radical and irrational. How far are we really supposed to go in loving our neighbors, in turning the other cheek, in giving to the poor, in believing for a healing? Didn't Jesus mention something about going the extra mile? I'm sorry if I keep restating the point, but our Christian faith is meant to take us out of our comfort zone in order to lead us to something greater than we've ever experienced.

Week 15: THE MILEAGE PEAK

Day 4 (Short Run, Speed Training 4 miles) ON TIRED LEGS

Run hard when it's hard to run. — *Paavo Nurmi, a legendary Olympic distance runner*[33]

I wake up groggy to the sound of my alarm. Still in a daze, I stick my legs out from under the blankets one by one and stretch by slowly moving my feet in circles. Once my heels hit the cold hardwood floor I become aware of the fatigue and tightness in my muscles. My training has reached its mileage peak and I feel it. Quietly, so not to wake up my sleeping family, I make myself some strong black tea and put on my running shoes. The cushioning in the soles of my sneakers is comforting to my aching feet. Once I get out in the fresh air I become more alert. I start my run feeling tired from the get go, but as I keep going, the tightness in my legs gradually decreases. After a few hills I feel like slowing down. Instead, I run even harder. I have found this strategy to be effective when I want to maintain my pace. It helps me persevere when I feel like stopping in the middle of my workout.

My Dear Marathoner, when your faith "mileage" increases you are often confronted by multiple long term challenges that require you to stand on what you believe without seeing immediate solutions and results. In these seasons of life it is easy to become emotionally weary and stop believing that God will bring answers in the middle or your spiritual battle. Resolve to say a firm "no" to the temptation to give up. Instead of allowing disappointment and discouragement to slow you down, push through even harder by spending extra time with Him and declaring His victory over the situations you are dealing with.

Week 15: THE MILEAGE PEAK

Day 5 (Short Run 3 miles) DON'T FORGET TO BREATHE

Consider how we can live off the CPR of God: as we believe, we inhale His words, and as we speak, we exhale His words. — Beth Moore, Believing God[34]

When I run I always breathe in on three steps and breathe out on two. It's like getting a deep breath in by three short inhales and letting a deep breath out in two short exhales. Breathing like this not only prevents me from getting out of breath but also reduces the chance of joint injury. By exhaling on alternating steps I ensure the impact of my landing switches from one leg to another. Before I learned how to do it, my right ankle got sore because I exhaled while landing mostly on my right leg and thus shifted more of my body weight on the right side. It took me a few runs to get used to the new breathing rhythm, but now it is second nature and it has definitely paid off.

Learning how to breathe properly is important in more than running. Breathing through contractions is one of the most important things they teach women preparing for childbirth. My husband once told me that deep diaphragmatic breathing is crucial in helping mixed martial arts fighters outlast their opponents. As followers of Christ we run, we fight and we give birth. We run the course God has prepared for us, we fight the enemy's schemes to get us off track and we help birth new lives into the Kingdom by sharing the message of salvation. So don't forget during your mileage peak to deeply inhale His Word and exhale it by praying it and speaking it over your circumstances. Each time you do it, His life circulates through your system.

Week 15: THE MILEAGE PEAK

Day 6 (Short Run 4 miles) POP IN THAT POWER GEL

Oh, praise the greatness of our God! — Deuteronomy 32:3b (NIV)

Some runners take special power gels to give them an extra boost for their performance, especially when running very long distances. I take those only on my highest mileage runs, and always one before and one during a marathon. These gels work by providing you with a concentrated "shot" of glucose and caffeine, and I noticed that they do make a difference if you can stomach them. In a spiritual sense, during your "mileage peaks" you need to get a much needed lift for especially exhausting seasons. So, pop in that "power gel" by starting your day with praise, worship, and thanksgiving even if you don't feel like it. Receive extra spiritual sustenance to get you through the toughest times. It's a kind of "gel" you can take as often as you want. Your strength will come back as Isaiah 40:30-31 promises: "Those who hope in the Lord will renew their strength. They will soar on wings like eagles; they will run and not grow weary, they will walk and not be faint."

Week 15: THE MILEAGE PEAK

Day 7 (Rest Day, Meditation) DETERMINED TO SUCCEED

The body doesn't want you to do this. As you run, it tells you to stop but the mind must be strong. You always go too far for your body. You must handle pain with strategy... It is not your age; it is not diet. It is the will to succeed. — Jacqueline Gareau, 1980 Boston Marathon Champion[35]

I have a friend who has been out of work for many months. He is a father of three with another baby on the way. He tells me I inspire him through my marathon training. I told him that he and his wife are *my* inspiration for persevering in the midst of difficulties. It takes courage to go through job loss and financial pressures and continue trusting God. I am sure it would be easy for me to feel like a failure in a situation like this; who wouldn't get discouraged? One important thing to keep in mind: my friend is not a failure just because his circumstances are failing right now.

My Dear Marathoner, your circumstances may not line up for a while, but you've accomplished your mileage peak if you've determined to succeed despite external resistance. Do not mistake your God-given victorious identity for a defeated mentality due to temporal disappointments. God has purposed your faith to succeed, so keep your eyes on Him at all times during those mileage peaks.

Meditation and prayer:

Whether you are in the midst of trial or blessing: you still need to have the true image of God in order to press on further than you've ever been and overcome anything that might lie in your path. Lord, what do You want to reveal to me about Yourself through my circumstances?

Week 16: A RUNNER'S HIGH

Day 1 (Long Run 15 miles) WHAT'S A RUNNER'S HIGH?

The antidote to stress and crisis is upgrading our fellowship with God. I must upgrade my relationship with Him, becoming more intimate than ever before. — Grahame Cooke, God Revealed[36]

The other day a friend who was trying to get in shape asked me if I knew how long he had to run in order to experience the runner's high. The question stumped me because I never recall a time in my running I could pinpoint and say, "this is the runner's high." I guess for me it's the feeling of being exhausted and then suddenly getting a second wind and wanting to run forever. It's the feeling of waking up before the sun groggy and out of it and then feeling wide awake and refreshed once I hit the running trail.

Is there a "runner's high" in spiritual life? I believe there is. It is when you encounter God in a place of intimacy and feel like you could never leave His presence. In those moments, you want to worship Him extravagantly and give Him your whole life. How do you get there? Just by being who you are in your commitment and desire for Him. Don't try to push yourself to run at a pace you can't sustain and be like somebody else. Set aside time to minister to God with your prayer, worship and reading the Word. Boldly approach God's throne and ask the Holy Spirit to minister to you.

One thing to keep in mind though is that the runner's high is not always there. I suspect that for many marathoners there are no endorphins or adrenaline left past mile 20. They just keep running because they've trained themselves to. In the same way, in real life we can't rely only on our feelings. The "high" moments are wonderful and life giving. They inspire us to keep training and we need to experience them as often as possible but we must be faithful to our call even when we aren't experiencing the feelings.

My Dear Marathoner, have you ever experienced a "runner's high" in your spiritual life? If yes, what was it like and what was your response to God in that moment? Do you still live by that response? If not, spend some time in prayer today asking the Holy Spirit to bring you to a closer intimacy with the Father and to renew your relationship with Him.

Week 16: A RUNNER'S HIGH

Day 2 *(Short Run 3 miles) IT BRINGS TRANSFORMATION*

My heart says of you, "Seek his face! Your face, Lord, I will seek."
— *Psalm 27:8 (NIV)*

A runner's high transforms the way you run. It revives and rejuvenates your form and pace, making you confident that you can keep going. Intimacy with the Lord, like a spiritual high, renews your affection for Him and strengthens your confidence in Him. You realize that despite the difficult terrain and all the mileage peaks you can successfully complete the race of life and fulfill His purposes. Your faith is renewed and strengthened by seeing His face. Continue to pursue fellowship with Him as much as you can and be open to the transformation it will bring.

Week 16: A RUNNER'S HIGH

Day 3 (Rest Day, Meditation) IT MAKES US RESPOND IN PRAISE

The Lord lives, praise be to my Rock! Exalted be my God, my Savior! — Psalm 18:46 (NIV)

My Dear Marathoner, find a place today where you can talk to God out loud. Start exalting His name. As His presence draws near, continue to lavish your worship on Him. Praise is such a natural response when you feel closeness with Him. Lord, You are worthy. God, You are powerful. You are greater than my circumstances. You hold my life in Your hands. Thank You for Your love. Thank You for Your abundant provision. Your presence is beautiful. My soul is being satisfied only by You. I love You and adore You.

Lift Him up to the proper place in your heart and in your words. Let the glory of His presence shine upon you like never before. Meditate on His majesty and goodness.

Week 16: A RUNNER'S HIGH

Day 4 (Short Run, Speed Training 5 miles) IT BRINGS REFRESHING

He who has compassion on them will guide them and lead them beside springs of water. — *Isaiah 49:10b (NIV)*

One of my running routes lies along a beautiful babbling brook. I can't tell you how many times after having run over 10 miles on some humid summer mornings I wished that I could have jumped in the cool water and drank from it like a dog. In all their wanderings the Israelites did not have the luxury of water bottles and Gatorade, so being close to springs of water was a matter of survival. God will cause us to experience the spiritual "runner's high" by refreshing us with the waters of His Spirit when we follow His guidance. His springs of life are just as essential for us spiritually as the water in the desert. There is only one way to quench your thirst in His Kingdom: just jump in and drink! You do it by openly receiving from Him without holding anything back. Here is my speed training challenge for you today: absorb every drop of His love into your heart. You can't bottle His presence up and carry it around for when you need it later. You need to learn to receive His love deep in your heart, so you can freely enter His presence at any time.

Week 16: A RUNNER'S HIGH

Day 5 (Short Run 4 miles) PLACE OF PEACE

You will keep in perfect peace him whose mind is steadfast, because he trusts in you. Trust in the Lord forever, for the Lord, the Lord, is the Rock eternal. — *Isaiah 26:3-4(NIV)*

The key to peace in each of our lives is submitting to God's authority through obedience. — *Beth Moore, Breaking Free*[37]

My Dear Marathoner, how do you find and maintain peace in this highly stressful culture? Isn't it hard not to feel rushed, overwhelmed and underachieved in the hectic daily pace of our lives? Your answer lies in submitting each area in your life to God by following Him. As you trust yourself into His hands and continue growing in your faith it is inevitable that the peace of God, like a runner's high, should gradually fill your soul beyond any natural understanding. Every area in your life that you surrender to God will be filled with His peace. Peace is not just an emotion. It is the absence of fighting, division, confusion, and torment in one's thoughts, feelings, and actions. It is God's *shalom*, which in Hebrew means "completeness, soundness, welfare, tranquility and contentment."[38] God's *shalom* in your life is a testimony of His sovereignty and greatness over any problem, issue or concern.

Week 16: A RUNNER'S HIGH

Day 6 (Short Run 5 miles) PLACE OF JOY

A cheerful heart is good medicine. — *Proverbs 17:22a*

Running a faith marathon gives you an opportunity to experience the "runner's high" in the form of joy. The Bible says you bear the fruit of joy as a result of His Spirit dwelling inside of you. Joy is a vital part of God's nature and we desperately need it to complete our race victoriously. If you've run through the valleys of pain before, God wants to direct your route through the valleys of rejoicing. Joy gives you strength to endure a long distance race. Ask God to fill you with His joy.

Week 16: A RUNNER'S HIGH

Day 7 (Rest Day, Meditation) *LOVING WITH ALL YOUR PASSION*

Love the Lord your God with all your heart and with all your soul and with all your mind and with all your strength. — Mark 12:30
(NIV)

Experts say the body's release of endorphins might be responsible for the runner's high phenomenon. These hormones are also told to be associated with love and passion. If our heart is where our passions spring up, then I am loving God by writing this devotional because I am passionate about encouraging others to step up to a place of encountering God. I am also loving Him with my strength because I literally use up and exhaust my physical energy while running. (Not to mention the late nights writing in front of the computer and my resulting sleep deprivation!) I have been loving Him with all my strength and mind by giving my all to running and writing during this training season. But even having poured it all out, I still have the stamina to keep going because of the passion that drives me to do this.

What are your passions? What are your strengths? What kinds of thoughts occupy your mind? How can you love God more with all of the above? Dream with Him and allow the Holy Spirit to form His desires within you that will ignite your passion.

Week 17: YOU'VE GOT IT!

DAY 1 (A Short "Long" Run 4 miles) A CRAMP IN MY SIDE

His divine power has given us everything we need for life and godliness through our knowledge of him who called us by his own glory and goodness. — 2 Peter 1:3 (NIV)

I've been looking forward to this week! After all the hard work it's time to celebrate what I've done, taper off and take it easy before the big day. The prescribed long run for this week doesn't seem to be long at all in comparison to previous weeks. After all, what's four miles after you've run twenty? That's what I thought yesterday before several stressful events unfolded in front of me in just one day. One of them involved a financial issue that hit me like a brick wall. I can tell you, I did not react like a super-spiritual person. I cried. I got angry. I did not sleep well. I needed to run today just to decompress. That's when the words of the title of this chapter stood bright and bold before my eyes: YOU'VE GOT IT! This is only a "4-mile run" of my faith training. I have trained sufficiently to overcome this situation in His victory. As I kept running, I mentally flipped through the pages of this devotional, thinking about the things I've written previously about trust, my Father's love, and perseverance. Yes, I've got it indeed.

Suddenly, something happened in the last two miles of my run that I've never experienced before in any of my marathon training. I got a bad cramp in my side that just wouldn't go away. A memory instantly came to my mind: as a kid, and even later as a teen, I always hated running because I would get painful side cramps almost every time I tried to run. Having a cramp like that used to be a good enough excuse for me to stop running, even if my gym grade depended on it. This sudden flashback helped me realize that God was trying to illustrate something through my cramp: reacting to financial stresses or any other difficulties without full trust in Him is like letting some pain in my side defeat me in my race. The mentality of lack is a thing of the past just like my annoying cramps. God is not lacking in His ability to provide anything good for my life. I have a choice to go on and believe that I've got what it takes to continue this race, or I can let the cramp of insecurity steal my joy and stop me in my tracks.

Here is a thought to meditate on: you've not only got it by now, but He has also got *you*!

Week 17: YOU'VE GOT IT!

Day 2 (Short Run 6 miles) KEEP IT GOING

But you, dear friends, build yourselves up in your most holy faith and pray in the Holy Spirit. Keep yourselves in God's love as you wait for the mercy of our Lord Jesus Christ to bring you to eternal life. — Jude 1:20-21 (NIV)

No striving is necessary. Just continue doing what you've been doing all along in this training: building yourself up in faith, praying and stepping out to share God's love with people around you. As Jude states in verse 24, Jesus is the one who is able to "keep you from falling and to present you before His (God's) glorious presence without fault and with great joy." Remember how during the first week we talked about running in such a way as to get a prize? Paul continues to develop this concept in Philippians 3. The prize is knowing Christ and the power of His resurrection, the sharing in His sufferings and becoming like Him in His death and resurrection (v. 10). Paul goes on to state that he does not consider himself to have attained that prize yet: "Forgetting what is behind and straining toward what is ahead, I press on toward the goal to win the prize for which God has called me heavenward in Christ Jesus" (v. 13). According to Paul, being driven by a Christ-centered goal is a sign of maturity (v. 15). The apostle encourages you to keep going. One day Jesus will joyfully bring you before God the Father. What a day it will be!

Week 17: YOU'VE GOT IT!

Day 3 (Rest Day, Meditation) YOU ARE A REFLECTION OF HIS DELIVERANCE

Moses answered the people, "Do not be afraid. Stand firm and you will see the deliverance the Lord will bring you today. The Egyptians you see today you will never see again. The Lord will fight for you; you need only to be still." — Exodus 14:13-14 (NIV)

Just as you have positioned your heart to run God's course by faith, He has positioned His mighty power to protect you and to fight for you. There are times to fight and advance but there are also important seasons when we need to be still and let Him contend for us. Stillness is possible only in a place of trust. It does not imply complete passivity: you need to "stand firm" and turn your complete attention to Him.

In what areas of your life has the enemy been attacking you? As you continue to stand firm in your faith by choosing to believe God's truth over the enemy's lies, the issues that have been bringing you down will start having less and less of an effect on your emotions, thoughts and actions. The deliverance and freedom that Christ secured for you on the cross will become more and more evident until you are running in its fullness.

Week 17: YOU'VE GOT IT

Day 4 (Short Run 4 miles, no speed training today) YOU ARE AN OVERCOMER

Count yourself dead to sin but alive to God in Christ Jesus. —
Romans 6:11 (NIV)

After being fixed for the second time my treadmill finally broke again. At this point, it is probably beyond cost efficient repair. It just couldn't take my persistent pounding anymore. The job of the running belt had been to provide resistance. I kept running until there was no resistance left. Sometimes you might feel like you are struggling against your own resistance and that your weaknesses and shortcomings are keeping you running in place. It is time to realize that you do not need to fight with yourself. Your sinful nature is dead and you are a new creation in Christ Jesus! Don't try to drag the old corpse with you to the race. There is an enemy of your soul that has been resisting you but he can't overcome your marathon-like perseverance that's based on what Christ did for you and who you are in Him. The enemy has not trained to run a long-distance course by faith like you have. As you continue to actively trust God mile after mile and become stronger and stronger, he will realize he can't beat you anymore.

My Dear Marathoner, run with freedom in your heart and without any self-blame as a new creation. Have confidence that you are an overcomer as a believer in Jesus Christ, "for everyone born of God overcomes the world. This is the victory that has overcome the world, even our faith. Who is it that overcomes the world? Only who believes that Jesus is the Son of God." (1 John 5:4-5)

Week 17: YOU'VE GOT IT

Day 5 (Short Run 4 miles) YOU ARE A LIGHT ON A HILL

You are the light of the world. A city that is set on a hill cannot be hidden... Let your light shine before men, that they may see your good works and glorify your Father in heaven. — Matthew 5:14-16 (NKJV)

When you run a race there are lots of spectators watching. Your results are posted on a website and sometimes even in a paper. You cannot hide your performance. Because God's life pulsates inside of you, your light shines brightly in the darkness of this world. Your life is a demonstration of God's goodness and the reality of God abiding among His people. When I turn the outside light on my porch in the evening all the bugs and moths in the neighborhood gather around it. That's what happens to hungry souls who are searching for the truth: they are drawn to you. It is hard not to recognize God's favor and grace upon your life. If you were to run a race at night, you would be the one to follow because you shine in the darkness and light up the path for everyone else.

Week 17: YOU'VE GOT IT

DAY 6 (Rest Day, Meditation) YOU ARE YOKED WITH HIM

Come to me, all you who labor and are heavy laden, and I will give you rest. Take My yoke upon you and learn from Me, for I am gentle and lowly at heart, and you will find rest for your souls. For My yoke is easy and My burden is light. — Matthew 11:28-30 (NKJV)

When I think of a yoke, I think of two hard working oxen bound together by a large wooden beam. They can walk only in the same direction. They share the weight of the load that they pull behind them. I wonder what it would be like if runners had to run their races while being paired like yoked oxen. I would hope the person yoked with me would be able to run the same pace and be strong enough to help with the haul. It blows my mind to think that Jesus is willing to be yoked with me in spite of my shortcomings! In fact, He urges me to join Him in His yoke because it will bring me rest. I can imagine that in order to put the yoke on I would need to bow my head down. It is a sign of humility and willingness to surrender. Once the yoke is on, I can only go where He goes. It's a yoke of partnership and friendship for a lifetime. I don't need to crumble under the weight of the world's and my own problems because I am carrying only the load that Jesus intended me to carry, and He's the one pulling all of the weight anyway.

My Dear Marathoner, throw off the heavy worldly burdens you've been carrying and take His yoke upon you instead. You have His promise that, no matter what tasks He calls you to take on, His burden is easy and His yoke is light. You will learn from Him and find the rest your soul needs even through your marathon-like tests of faith.

Week 17: YOU'VE GOT IT

Day 7 (Short Run, 2 miles) YOU ARE HIS VICTORIOUS BRIDE

Who is this coming up from the desert leaning on her lover?
— Song of Solomon 8:5 (NIV)

In Song of Solomon, the beloved Shulamite says to her Lover: "Draw me after you and let us run together!" (SS 1:4, NASB) I hope this faith training became a process of God drawing your soul and coming to a place of intimacy with Him you've never experienced before. This is a good time to say, "I have run after You, God. You truly are the Lover of my Soul. Let us run together!"

My Dear Marathoner, as you go through the training and testing of your faith, you reach a level of maturity and grow into the image of the victorious bride Jesus is passionately in love with. When you respond to His love by sticking to your commitment and run after Him no matter what, your faith evolves past the infatuated stage of "My beloved is mine and I am his" to a sacrificial and selfless response, "I belong to my lover." (SS 7:10) Notice that the second part of that verse says "and his desire is for me." You are His desire and passion. The Lover is attracted to the maturity and strength that His Beloved exemplifies: "You are beautiful, my darling, as Tirzah, lovely as Jerusalem, majestic as troops with banners." In times of testing, you can come victoriously out of the desert places in your life, leaning on your Lover. So let Him draw you, and keep running with Him in the fullness of His glory.

YOUR BIG DAY (26.2!)

Take it like a marathoner

Once I hated running because of the discomfort it brought but today I am part of an anxious crowd in downtown Pittsburgh that is shivering from the early morning chill and adrenaline rush, ready to set off on a long-distance race through the "City of Bridges." I am not feeling that great because of a head cold but I am determined to run nonetheless. I've come too far to quit; I've trained for too long to turn away. The anthem is sung, the gun has fired and I finally cross the starting line. I start a little slow, navigating among the runners, trying to find clear openings so I can accelerate. I quickly find my pace and enjoy the run while taking in the exciting atmosphere all around me. After the first half of the course, the route is becoming less scenic and more challenging. After I've scaled "Cardiac Hill" I start feeling weaker, probably because of my cold. But I just grab some orange slices from volunteers and tell myself "take it like a marathoner." I progressively grow more tired, and the sun is mercilessly beating down overhead. I just pour a cup of water on my head and tell myself "take it like a marathoner." After mile 20 I see a lot of people stop running and starting to walk, and when the city line appears around the bend it seems like it is still 26.2 miles away. Talk about discomfort. But I just continue telling myself to take it like a marathoner and keep going, thanking God for some down hill relief. During the final mile I find some shade on the side of the road and keep praying that the Lord gives me the strength to make it without passing out. Finally, I come around the corner and see the finish line. It's the most rewarding sight. I dart for it with all my remaining strength and finish at 3:55:22. It's the first time I've broken the four-hour barrier in my running career. I know I've trained hard, but I still believe I accomplished something beyond my natural ability because God's hand was upon me during the race.

My Dear Marathoner, the hand of God is upon your race, whether it is physical or spiritual. I hope that by now you see yourself as a supernatural runner and tell yourself to take life's challenges like a faith marathoner.

The Post-Race Recovery

We ought always to thank God for you, brothers, and rightly so, because your faith is growing more and more, and the love everyone of you has for each other is increasing... We constantly pray for you, that our God may count you worthy of his calling, and that by his power he may fulfill every good purpose of yours and every act prompted by your faith. We pray this so that the name of our Lord Jesus may be glorified in you, and you in him, according to the grace of our God and the Lord Jesus Christ. — 2 Thessalonians 1:3, 11-12 (NIV)

After running the marathon and completing this book, I still ask myself, "How does our faith grow?" Jesus said that nothing is impossible to the one whose faith is like a mustard seed (Matthew 17:20). Mustard seeds are tiny. I recently learned that they germinate extremely quickly and can sprout overnight. They grow on their own with plenty of sunshine and do not require much cultivating by human hands. The point that Jesus was making is that a mustard plant grows very large compared to the size of its seed. Just like a mustard seed, our faith was meant to grow rapidly. We can't make it sprout other than to provide favorable conditions, such as fertile soil (being willing for God to work in us) and lots of sun (spending time in His presence and letting His light shine on us). After that, we just need to keep up with the increasing size of our faith by renewing our minds and by putting it into practice. To give a running illustration, I already had faith that I could run a marathon. I just needed to train my body so it would catch up to the size of my faith.

As you exercise your faith by stepping out and acting on it, the Kingdom of God also expands. Heaven's reality increases in our daily lives. God's Kingdom, just like our faith, begins with a small seed. Once it is planted in the field of our lives it is meant to grow into something significant. Our faith and the expression of His Kingdom in our lives grow hand-in-hand. As a result, there is nothing impossible for us because our life's purpose and calling are being fulfilled.

After a week of rest and recovery from the marathon I looked at the longest hill of my training route as I passed it in the car and said to my husband: "I think that hill is calling my name." If I take time off from running for too long I go through a withdrawal. My Dear Marathoner, after completing this faith training I hope you realize that, just like me, you will never be the same. Without pursuing His purpose you'll go through a withdrawal too. You have become a supernatural runner with a faith that's ready to overcome. Running after God's purposes has become your natural state. Approaching life differently than living by faith will seem strange to you after you've tried it. You can do this faith training over and over again, applying it to different areas of your life and becoming continually stronger. It was an honor to train and grow with you. I wish you many more fulfilling and successful runs throughout your life of faith. I will be happy to hear your training story that you can share by connecting with me through Beginner Marathoner's Faith Training Facebook page.

ENDNOTE

[1] Thinkexist.com website, accessed July 12, 2012, taken from http://www.thinkexist.com/quotes/roger_bannister; s. v. "Roger Bannister quotes"

[2] NIV – Scripture taken from the Holy Bible, New International Version®. Copyright © 1973, 1978, 1984 by International Bible Society. Used by permission of Zondervan Publishing House. All rights reserved. Bible quotes in this text are taken from the NIV unless otherwise specified.

[3] Rick Warren, *The Purpose Driven Life.* (Grand Rapids, Michigan: Zondervan, 2002), 198

[4] NKJV – Scripture taken from the New King James Version. Copyright © 1979, 1980, 1982 by Thomas Nelson, Inc. Used by permission. All rights reserved

[5] Beth Moore, *James. Mercy Triumphs* (Nashville, Tennessee: Life Way Press, 2011), 11

[6] Brainyquote.com website, accessed July 12, 2012, taken from http://www.brainyquote.com/quotes/authors/p/pat_riley.html; s. v. "Pat Riley quotes"

[7] Bill Johnson, Kris Vallotton, *The Supernatural Ways of Royalty* (Shippensburg, Pennsylvania: Destiny Image Publishers, Inc, 2006), 41

[8] August, Chris/Cash, Ed. "7x70." Lyrics. Perf. Chris August. No Far Away. Chris August, Ed Cash, 2010

[9] Blue Letter Bible. "Dictionary and Word Search for "sin" in the NKJV." Blue Letter Bible 1996-2012. 6 January 2012. Strong's Hebrew, accessed January 6, 2012, taken from http://www.blueletterbible.org/search/translationResultscfm?Criteria=sin&t=NKJV&sf=5; s. v. "sin." Hebrew Strong's Number H2398

[10] Henry T. Blackaby, Claude V. King, *Experiencing God. Knowing and Doing the Will of God* (Nashville, Tennessee: Life Way Press 1990), 13

[11] http://www.youtube.com/watch?v=768IV_WO4ec posted by magicman808, accessed March 12, 2013, s. v. "Heather Dorniden"

[12] http://www.youtube.com/watch?v=kZ1XWp6vFdE&feature=related posted by necessity4failure, accessed March 25, 2012, s. v. "Derek Redmond"

[13] Rick Moore, *Big Fish Big Pond,* accessed March 25, 2012, taken from http://www1.umn.edu/news/features/2009/UR_CONTENT_115226.htm , s. v. "Heather Dorniden"

[14] Rick Moore, *Big Fish Big Pond,* accessed March 25, 2012, taken from http://www1.umn.edu/news/features/2009/UR_CONTENT_115226.htm , s. v. "Heather Dorniden"

[15] Motivational Quotes for Women website, accessed March 25, 2012, taken from http://www.motivational-quotes-for-women.com, s. v. "running motivational quotes"

[16] Graham, Brennan. *You Raise Me Up*, Lyrics. Perf. Josh Groban. Closer. David Foster, 2004

[17] Motivational Quotes for Women website, accessed March 25, 2012, taken from http://www.motivational-quotes-for-women.com, s. v. "running motivational quotes"

[18] Bill Johnson, *The Supernatural Power of a Transformed Mind* (Shippensburg, Pennsylvania: Destiny Image Publishers, Inc. 2005), 66

[19] Blue Letter Bible. "Dictionary and Word Search for "revelation" in the NIV." Blue Letter Bible. 1996-2012. 13 Jul 2012. http://www.blueletterbible.org/search/translationResults.cfm?Criteria=%22revelaion%22&t=NIV. Greek Strong's Number G602.

[20] Bill Johnson, *The Supernatural Power of a Transformed Mind* (Shippensburg, Pennsylvania: Destiny Image Publishers, Inc. 2005), 153-154

[21] Riva, Oliviero/Finazzi, Massimo. "Legacy." Lyrics. Perf. Nicole Nordeman. Woven and Spun. Hal Leonard Music Publishing, 2002

[22] *Courageous*. Dir. Alex Kendrick. Perf. Ben Davies and Ken Bevel. TriStar, 2011

[23] Beth Moore, *Believing God* (Nashville, Tennessee: Life Way Press, 2004), 111

[24] Brainyquote.com website, accessed August 1, 2012, taken from http://www.brainyquote.com/quotes/authors/n/newt_gingrich_2.html, s. v. "perseverance quotes"

[25] Meb Keflezighi, with Dick Patrick, *Run to Overcome: The Inspiring Story of an American Champion's Long Distance Quest to Achieve a Big Dream* (Carolstream, Illinois: Tyndale House Publishers, Inc. 2010), the Kindle Edition

[26] Motivational Quotes for Women website, accessed March 6, 2012, taken from http://www.motivational-quotes-for-women.com, s. v. "perseverance quotes"

[27] Motivational Quotes for Women website, accessed March 6, 2012, taken from http://www.motivational-quotes-for-women.com, s. v. "perseverance quotes"

[28] Kris Vallotton, *Spirit Wars. Winning the Invisible Battle Against Sin and the Enemy* (Minneapolis, Minnesota: Chosen Books, a division of Baker Publishing Group 2012), 55

[29] *The Lion King.* Dir. Roger Allers and Rob Minkoff. Perf. James Earl Jones (as Mufasa). Disney, 1994

[30] Blue Letter Bible. "Dictionary and Word Search for "workmanship" in the NIV." Blue Letter Bible. 1996-2012. 4 Apr 2012. http://www.blueletterbible.org.search/translationResults.cfm?Criteria= workmanship&t=NIV&sf=5 Hebrew Strong's Number H4399

[31] Bill Johnson, Kris Vallotton, *The Supernatural Ways of Royalty* (Shippensburg, Pennsylvania: Destiny Image Publishers, Inc, 2006), 147

[32] NASB – Scripture taken from the New American Standard Bible®, Copyright© 1960, 1962, 1963, 1968, 1971, 1972, 1973, 1975, 1977, 1995 by the Lockman Foundation. Used by permission. www.Lockman.org

[33] Wild Cats Youth Cross Country Team website, accessed March 6, 2012, taken from http://www.wildcats.rockriver.net/quotes.html, s. v. "running quotes"

[34] Beth Moore. *Believing God* (Nashville, Tennessee: LifeWay Press, 2004), 115

[35] Inspirational Quotes and Quotations, accessed March 6, 2012, taken from http://www.inspirational-quotes-and-quotations.com/inspirational-running-quotes.html, s. v. "running quotes"

[36] Graham Cooke. *God Revealed* (Grand Rapids, Michigan: Chosen Books, a division of Baker Publishing Group, 2003, 2005), 27

[37] Beth Moore. *Breaking Free. Making Liberty in Christ a Reality in Life* (Nashville, Tennessee: LifeWay Press, 1999), 216

[38] Blue Letter Bible. "Dictionary and Word Search for "peace" in the NIV." Blue Letter Bible. 1996-2012, 20 June 2012. http://www.blueletterbible.org.search/translationResults.cfm?Criteria=peace&t=NIV&sf=5 Hebrew Strong's Number H7965